W9-BKK-545

Family Treasures

Family Treasures

✦

Creating Strong Families

John DeFrain
Extension Family and Community
Development Specialist
University of Nebraska–Lincoln

And the
University of Nebraska–Lincoln
For Families Writing Team

iUniverse, Inc.
New York Lincoln Shanghai

Family Treasures
Creating Strong Families

Copyright © 2007 by The Board of Regents of the University of Nebraska on behalf of the University of Nebraska-Lincoln Extension

All rights reserved. No part of this book may be used or reproduced by any means, graphic, electronic, or mechanical, including photocopying, recording, taping or by any information storage retrieval system without the written permission of the publisher except in the case of brief quotations embodied in critical articles and reviews.

iUniverse books may be ordered through booksellers or by contacting:

iUniverse
2021 Pine Lake Road, Suite 100
Lincoln, NE 68512
www.iuniverse.com
1-800-Authors (1-800-288-4677)

Because of the dynamic nature of the Internet, any Web addresses or links contained in this book may have changed since publication and may no longer be valid.

ISBN: 978-0-595-45886-8 (pbk)
ISBN: 978-0-595-90187-6 (ebk)

Printed in the United States of America

The views expressed in this work are solely those of the author and do not necessarily reflect the views of the publisher, and the publisher hereby disclaims any responsibility for them.

University of Nebraska–Lincoln Extension helps people put knowledge to work. It provides a wide range of educational opportunities, delivered in a variety of venues, so participants have knowledge they can use to make sound decisions to better their lives. Extension educators and specialists teach, facilitate and collaborate in providing research-based information to Nebraskans. For more information about University of Nebraska–Lincoln Extension, visit the Web site at: http://www.extension.unl.edu. For more information about the UNL for Families Extension Team, or to order additional copies of *Family Treasures—Creating Strong Families*, visit the UNL for Families Web site: http://unlforfamilies.unl.edu.

Extension is a Division of the Institute of Agriculture and Natural Resources at the University of Nebraska–Lincoln cooperating with the Counties and the United States Department of Agriculture.

University of Nebraska–Lincoln Extension educational programs abide with the nondiscrimination policies of the University of Nebraska–Lincoln and the United States Department of Agriculture.

Contents

This book on creating strong families of all kinds was created by a statewide team of University of Nebraska–Lincoln Extension specialists and educators whose work focuses on the positive development of children, youth and families. This UNL for Families team was recently given an Annie E. Casey Foundation/4-H Youth Development Strengthening Families Award for its efforts.

Lead Authors

- John DeFrain, Extension Specialist, Family and Community Development

- University of Nebraska–Lincoln For Families Writing Team

  Gail Brand, Extension Educator, Seward County

  Ann Fenton, Extension Educator, Pierce County

  Jeanette Friesen, Extension Educator, Hamilton County

  Janet Hanna, Extension Educator, Garfield, Loup and Wheeler Counties

  Kathleen Lodl, Extension Specialist, 4-H Youth Development

  Mary Nelson, Extension Educator, Douglas/Sarpy Counties

  Lee Sherry, Extension Educator, Madison County

Contributing Authors

Brenda Aufdenkamp	Alice Henneman	Sandy Preston
Kim Bearnes	May Ann Holland	Barb Schmidt
Linda Boeckner	Eileen Krumbach	Carol Schwarz
Kathy Bosch	Mary Loftis	Cindy Strasheim
Myrna DuBois	Carla Mahar	Dianne Swanson
Jackie Farrell	Leanne Manning	Stephanie Thorson
Cheryl Fisher	Jeanne Murray	Ruth Vonderohe
Marilyn Fox	Lynne Osborn	Cathy Weaver
Connie Francis	Carol Plate	LaDonna Werth
Sondra Germer	Darlene Pohlman	Lorrie Wold

Designer and Editor:

Gary Goodding, Designer
Linda Ulrich, Editor
Communications and Information Technology

Introduction

Why Are Strong Families so Important?

The late David R. Mace, a pioneer in the field of marriage and family enrichment, was fond of saying, "Nothing in the world could make human life happier than to greatly increase the number of happy couples and strong families."

We agree with him, and for that reason we applaud the work being done in countless places and countless ways around the world to strengthen and support families. Families, in all the diverse patterns, sizes, creeds and colors they come in, are, indeed, the heart and soul of all human societies.

Families are perhaps society's oldest and most resilient institutions. From the beginning of human life, people have grouped themselves into families to find emotional, physical and collective support. Although in recent years social commentators have predicted the demise of both marriage and the family, they not only survive but continue to change and evolve. Family structures may vary around the world, and yet, the value of *family* endures. And even though divorce statistics continue to run high in the United States and other countries, people still bond into couples and seek the long-term commitment that marriage promises, even if it does not always deliver.

Families are the basic, foundational social units in society. Therefore, healthy individuals within healthy families are at the core of a healthy society. The late Carl Whitaker, a world-renowned family therapist, argued that there are, in effect, no individuals in the world. Only fragments of families. If we believe this, it is in everyone's best interest to help create a positive environment for all families. This can be a labor of love for all of our social institutions: educational institutions, businesses, human and family service agencies, religious institutions, the military, health organizations, literally everyone involved in the daily life of a community.

Families are our most intimate social environment. They are the places where we begin the vital processes of socializing our children: teaching them—in partnership with countless others in the community—how to survive and thrive in the world.

1

Sometimes marriages get lost in all of the hubbub surrounding modern life. We attend to the children's needs. We make the boss happy at work. But we often let our own personal health and well-being slide, and we borrow time and energy from our marriages to satisfy other demands in our world. The problem with this is that a healthy marriage is at the heart of a healthy two-parent family. We are reminded of the saying, "The best thing a father can do for his children is to love their mother."

Of course, there are countless single-parent families that are strong, emotionally healthy, and deserving of respect and support. And it also is important for communities to find creative ways to strengthen and support two-parent families and make it possible for fathers to enjoy the benefits of increased time and involvement with their children. Moms shouldn't have to carry all the burdens of child rearing alone. And dads shouldn't miss all the wonderful feelings a parent experiences watching one's children grow and learn. As one young father noted, "It's just so much fun to be with my kids. I'm always thinking, 'What are they going to do next?' They're so unpredictable and interesting."

Life in families can bring us great joy or excruciating pain, depending upon how well family relationships are going. A healthy marriage and family can be a valuable resource for helping us endure difficulties that life inevitably brings. On the other hand, unhealthy or dysfunctional relationships can create terrible problems that may persist from one generation to the next.

The International Family Strengths Perspective

A Summary

- Families, in all their remarkable diversity, are the basic foundation of human cultures.

- All families have strengths. If one looks only for problems in a family, one will see only problems.

- It's not about structure, it's about function.

- Strong marriages are the center of many strong families.

- Strong families tend to produce great kids; and a good place to look for great kids is in strong families.

- If you grew up in a strong family as a child, it will probably be easier for you to create a strong family of your own as an adult.

- The relationship between money and family strengths is shaky, at best.

- Strengths develop over time.

- Strengths are often developed in response to challenges.

- Strong families don't tend to think much about their strengths, they just live them.

- Strong families, like people, are not perfect.

- When seeking to unite groups of people, communities, and even nations, uniting around the cause of strengthening families—a cause we can all sanction—can be a powerful strategy.

- Human beings have the right and responsibility to feel safe, comfortable, happy, and loved. Strong families are where this all happens.

Looking at Life From a Strengths-based Perspective

The family strengths perspective is a world-view or orientation toward life and families, grounded in research with more than 24,000 family members in 28 countries around the world. It is basically a positive, optimistic orientation. It does not ignore family problems but restores them to their proper place in life: as vehicles for testing our capacities as families and reaffirming our vital human connections with each other.

Over the past three decades researchers at the University of Nebraska–Lincoln led by John DeFrain, the University of Alabama-Tuscaloosa led by Nick Stinnett, the University of Minnesota-St. Paul led by David H. Olson, and affiliated institutions in the United States and around the world have studied families from a strengths-based perspective. Research on strong families has not only resulted in models for better understanding the qualities of strong families; it has also suggested a number of propositions that have importance in how we look at families in general, and how we can successfully live in our own families. (For detailed information on the research, see *More About Couple and Family Research* at the end of this book.)

The family strengths perspective evolves over time as our understanding of strong families increases. It is not a static set of ideas or rigorously testable hypotheses, but more like a family itself: a constantly growing and changing dialogue about the nature of strong marriages and strong families. Over the past three decades, researchers looking at couples and families from a strengths perspective have developed a number of propositions derived from their work around the world that we believe merit serious consideration:

- Families, in all their remarkable diversity, are the basic foundation of human cultures. Strong families are critical to the development of strong communities, and strong communities promote and nurture strong families.

- All families have strengths. And, all families have challenges and areas of potential growth. If one looks only for problems in a family, one will see only problems. If one also looks for strengths, one will find strengths.

- It's not about structure, it's about function. When talking about families, it is common to make the mistake of focusing on external family structure or type of family rather than internal family functioning. There are strong single-parent families, strong stepfamilies, strong nuclear families, strong extended families, strong families with gay and lesbian members, and strong two-parent families.

- Strong marriages are the center of many strong families. The couple relationship is an important source of strength in many families with children who are doing well. Parents—both fathers and mothers—cannot afford to neglect their relationship with each other, and it is important to find ways to nurture positive couple relationships for the good of everyone in the family.

- Strong families tend to produce great kids; and a good place to look for great kids is in strong families (Stinnett & O'Donnell, 1996).

- If you grew up in a strong family as a child, it will probably be easier for you to create a strong family of your own as an adult. But, it's also quite possible to do so if you weren't so lucky and grew up in a seriously troubled family (DeFrain, Jones, Skogrand, & DeFrain, 2003).

- The relationship between money and family strengths is shaky, at best. Once a family has adequate financial resources—and adequate is a slippery and subjective word to define—the relentless quest for more and more money is not likely to increase the family's quality of life, happiness together, or the strength of their relationships with each other. Rampant materialism in Western culture can be a dead end, for as our couples and families over the years have told us clearly, "The best things in life are not things."

- Strengths develop over time. When couples start out in life together, they sometimes have considerable difficulty adjusting to each other, and these difficulties are quite predictable. Adjusting to each other is not an easy task. Many couples who are unstable at first end up creating a healthy, happy family.

- Strengths are often developed in response to challenges. A couple and family's strengths are tested by life's everyday stressors and also by the significant crises that all of us face sooner or later. For many couples and families it takes several years before they believe they have become a strong family, and they know this because they have been tested over time and tested by fire, by the significant challenging events that life inevitably brings.

- Strong families don't tend to think much about their strengths, they just live them. These families often respond much like the baseball player who is asked how he hits home runs: "Well, I just take this bat and swing it at the ball when it comes in." It is, however, useful to carefully examine a family's strengths and discuss precisely how family members use them to great advantage.

- Strong families, like people, are not perfect. Even in the strongest of families we can sometimes be like porcupines: prickly, disagreeable, eager and ready to enjoy conflict with each other. But we also have a considerable need to cuddle up with each other for warmth and support in the darkest hours, for human beings deep down are genuinely social beings. Tapping into Chinese wisdom, we quote the ancient sage who argued that, "It is easier to rule a country than regulate a family" (National Geographic Society, 1995). A strong family is a piece of art continually in progress, always in the process of growing and changing.

- When seeking to unite groups of people, communities, and even nations, uniting around the cause of strengthening families—a cause we can all sanction—can be a powerful strategy. Ethnic and cultural groups often squabble and war over their differences, but the realization that families are the foundation for all our groups, and the strengths of families are remarkably similar from group to group, gives us powerful common ground for working together.

- Human beings have the right and responsibility to feel safe, comfortable, happy, and loved. Strong families are where this all happens.

What Is a Strong Family, Anyway?

One question that has fascinated researchers in the field of family studies for many years is, "What constitutes a strong family?" In essence, what are the qualities that make for success in families? What are the qualities that make for success in marriages? Finding an answer to this question is important, because with this foundation of knowledge we can help people learn about marital and family strengths and offer them the information necessary to create their own strong family.

Research at the University of Nebraska–Lincoln for more than 30 years has focused on families in the United States and around the world who believe they are doing well. Information has been gathered, through in-depth family interviews, observations and written questionnaires of more than 24,000 family members, from all 50 states in this country and 27 other countries around the world. Amazingly, when you ask people around the globe, "What makes your family strong?" the answers are remarkably similar from culture to culture. Our model of family strengths has six major qualities:

Appreciation and affection for each other

People in strong families deeply care for one another, and they let each other know this on a regular basis. They are not afraid to express their love.

Commitment

Members of strong families show a strong commitment to one another, investing time and energy in family activities. They do not allow their work or other priorities to take too much time away from family interaction. Family members are also committed to each other's personal growth as a means of strengthening the family as a whole.

Positive communication

Successful families are often task-oriented in their communication, identifying problems and discussing how to solve them together. Perhaps even more important than this, however, strong families also spend time talking with and listening to one another just to stay connected. Some of the most important talk occurs when no one is working at connection: open-ended, rambling conversations can reveal important information that helps smooth out the bumps of family living.

Enjoyable time together

We have asked literally thousands of people, "What are your happiest memories from childhood?" The vast majority tell us about family times together. Few reply that money, cars, fancy homes, television sets or elaborate and expensive vacations make a happy family and are part of their fondest memories. Strong and happy families are ones that do things together, families that genuinely enjoy the times they share with each other.

Spiritual well-being

Religion or spirituality also can be important to strong marriages and families. Spiritual well-being describes this concept, indicating that it can include organized religion, but not necessarily so. People describe this in a variety of ways: Some talk about faith in God, hope or a sense of optimism in life; some say they feel a oneness with the world. Others talk about their families in almost religious terms, describing the love they feel for one another with a great deal of reverence. Others express these kinds of feelings in terms of ethical values and commitment to important causes. Spiritual well-being can be seen as the caring center within each individual that promotes sharing, love and compassion.

The ability to manage stress and crisis effectively

Finally, strong marriages and families are not immune to stress and crisis, but they are not as crisis-prone as troubled families tend to be. Rather, they possess the ability to manage both daily stressors and difficult life crises creatively and effectively. They know how to prevent trouble before it happens and how to work together to meet challenges when they inevitably occur in life.

What About Love?

We are occasionally asked about love: Where does it fit in the family strengths model?

In our earlier models of family strengths, we viewed all of the family strengths in a circular fashion—all intertwined, highly related and essentially inseparable—and we placed the concept of love in the center. This model works well for cultures where love is a central concept. In fact, when a researcher asks many Americans about the strengths of their families, love is likely to be cited many times.

We see love as both a feeling one has for others, and as loving actions that human beings demonstrate regularly toward each other. Loving actions toward each other lead to warm and loving feelings, and these feelings lead to loving actions in a reciprocal process. Though an abusive spouse may say "I love you," words without loving actions are meaningless.

When people across the country and around the world describe the qualities that make their family strong, these are some of the traits they talk about:

Appreciation and Affection
Caring for each other
Friendship
Respect for individuality
Playfulness
Humor

Commitment
Trust
Honesty
Dependability
Faithfulness
Sharing

Positive Communication
Giving compliments
Sharing feelings
Avoiding blame
Being able to compromise
Agreeing to disagree

Enjoyable Time Together
Quality time in great quantity
Good things take time
Enjoying each other's company
Simple good times
Sharing fun times

Spiritual Well-being
Hope
Faith
Compassion
Shared ethical values
Oneness with humankind

The Ability to Manage Stress and Crisis Effectively
Adaptability
Seeing crises as challenges and opportunities
Growing through crises together
Openness to change
Resilience

The Qualities of Strong Families

Assessing Couple and Family Strengths

Perhaps the best way to understand the qualities that make families strong is to think about your own couple and family relationships. As you read this book, you can assess relationship strengths in your family and see how other family members perceive your strengths as a group. You also will have the opportunity to build upon some of your strengths to become a stronger family.

Since human beings tend to be problem-oriented in their thinking—meaning that we tend to focus on problems and think about solutions—we are not very likely to think how good things are, in general, and how good things are in our marriages and families, in particular. This, however, can be a very useful exercise because oftentimes we forget how much we mean to each other, we forget to be thankful for each other, we forget how our families are the foundation for our lives.

If all this makes sense to you, fill out the American Family Strengths Inventory© (AFSI) that is presented in the next sections of this book. For example, before reading the section on *Appreciation and Affection for Each Other*, take a few minutes to see how you think you're doing on this as a couple and/or family in this dimension. You then can discuss your responses to the items, and talk about the strengths you demonstrate with each other and the areas of potential growth you would like to enhance. A planning guide is included so you can develop goals related to each strength. At the end of the discussion on each strength, there are a variety of tried and true activities for increasing that particular strength. These activities have been tested by many couples and families and have been judged to be effective ways to strengthen relationships. Some are geared toward your family, others are specifically for couples. The book was created for both single-parent and two-parent families. Most of the activities can be adjusted to meet the needs of your family, whatever its composition. Be creative! You might even think about involving grandparents, significant others or other people important in your life. We encourage you to read through these activities and do some of them with your mate and your family. We believe you'll like the results.

9

American Family Strengths Inventory©

Research with more than 24,000 family members in the United States and around the world has found that strong families have a wide variety of qualities that contribute to the family members' sense of personal worth and feelings of satisfaction in their relationships with each other. The American Family Strengths Inventory included in the six sections throughout this book works well with couples and families in the United States and other English-speaking cultures.

One of the first steps in developing the strengths of one's family is to assess those areas in which the family is doing well and those areas in which family members would like to grow further.

Family members doing this exercise will be able to identify those areas they would like to work on together to improve and those areas of strength that will serve as the foundation for their growth and positive change together.

This American Family Strengths Inventory has been validated through research with more than 24,000 family members in the United States and 27 other countries around the world. These studies of family strengths have been conducted since 1974 by Nick Stinnett, John DeFrain and their many colleagues.

References:

DeFrain, J. (1999). Strong families around the world. *Family Matters: Australian Institute of Family Studies*, 53 (Winter), 6-13.

DeFrain, J., & Stinnett, N. (2002). Family strengths. In J.J. Ponzetti et al. (Eds.), *International encyclopedia of marriage and family* (2nd ed.). New York: Macmillan Reference Group, 637-642.

Olson, D.H., & DeFrain, J. (2006). *Marriages and families: Intimacy, diversity, and strengths* (5th ed.). New York: McGraw-Hill.

Stinnett, N., & DeFrain, J. (1985). *Secrets of strong families*. Boston: Little, Brown.

Researchers:

John DeFrain, Ph.D., professor and University of Nebraska–Lincoln Extension Family and Community Development Specialist, Department of Family and Consumer Sciences, College of Education and Human Sciences, Institute of Agriculture and Natural Resources, University of Nebraska–Lincoln, 254 Mabel Lee Hall, Lincoln, Nebraska 68588-0236. Phone: (402) 472-1659 or (402) 472-2957. E-mail: jdefrain1@unl.edu.

Nick Stinnett, Ph.D., Professor, Department of Human Development and Family Studies, University of Alabama, Tuscaloosa, Alabama. Phone: (205) 348-7864. E-mail: nstinne1@ches.

©Copyrighted material. For nonprofit educational purposes only. Not for resale.

Appreciation and Affection for Each Other

Before reading the next section, think about how you show appreciation and affection to your spouse and other family members. Take the following assessment to see how you are doing. You can then discuss your responses to the items, and talk about the strengths you demonstrate with each other and talk about where you would like to improve. A planning guide is included so you can develop some goals.

American Family Strengths Inventory©

Appreciation and Affection for Each Other

Family members can record their perceptions here in the area of *Appreciation and Affection for Each Other*. Feel free to make copies of this page for each member of your family or use the additional copies of this Inventory in the Appendix. Once each member has completed the Inventory, record their responses on the Tally Sheet provided in the Appendix.

You may want to complete this survey now, then again in three months and again in another six months. That way, you can see how your family is progressing.

Put an "S" for Strength beside the qualities you feel your family has achieved and a "G" beside those qualities that are an area of potential Growth. If the particular characteristic does not apply to your family or is not a characteristic that is important to you, put an "NA" for Not Applicable.

After recording your perceptions, spend some enjoyable time talking together about how your views are similar and how they are different. Remember: No one is absolutely right and no one is absolutely wrong on this. Everyone has a valid perception of what is happening and their views need to be considered carefully and respectfully.

Family Member's Name:_____ Date:_____

In Our Family ...

We appreciate each other and let each other know this. _____

We enjoy helping each other. _____

We are good at keeping our promises to each other. _____

We like to show affection to each other. _____

We feel close to each other. _____

We like to be kind to each other. _____

We like to hug each other. _____

We enjoy being thoughtful toward each other. _____

We wait for each other without complaining. _____

We give each other enough time to complete necessary tasks.   _____

We grow stronger because we love each other.   _____

All things considered, we have appreciation and affection for each other.   _____

© Copyrighted material. For nonprofit educational purposes only. Not for resale.

Our Plan for Increasing Appreciation and Affection for Each Other

Now that you know your family's strengths related to appreciation and affection, read the next section of the book. As you read, you may want to think about how the examples fit your family. You can then look at ways your family members might strengthen their appreciation and affection for each other and write them in the space below. The activities at the end of this section are there to help you get started.

Our Plan

Based on our discussion about Appreciation and Affection for Each Other, *we have decided to do the following things in the coming weeks and months to enhance this quality in our family:*

1. _____

_____

_____

_____

2. _____

_____

_____

_____

3. _____

_____

_____

_____

Signed: _____   _____

_____   _____

_____   _____

Positive Emotional Bonds

If we were to use one word to describe families, we would choose the word emotion. Families are about emotion. When you are focusing on strong families, you are talking about positive emotional bonds and how we create these with each other.

Family therapists can tell you about what it feels like to walk into a roomful of family members who are angry with each other. It often can feel like the hair on the back of your neck is going to stand up. The hostility seems to give a dangerous electrical charge to the environment. Everyone can feel it, almost instinctively.

Likewise, when you walk into a roomful of family members who have genuine appreciation and affection for each other, there is something in the air: a warm, fuzzy, indescribable feeling that fills the family's world with a positive glow. People in strong families care deeply for each other and let each other know this on a regular basis. They feel good about each other and know how important it is to continually express these feelings.

One divorcing husband told us, "She cooked dinner every evening, but it never occurred to me to thank her for it. She didn't thank me for going to work every day." But we can't afford to take loved ones for granted and giving sincere thanks builds a positive atmosphere where bonds of emotional connection are nurtured.

Interviews with families in our research have led us to "guesstimate" that the ratio of positive to negative interchanges in strong families may reach the 10-to-1 or even 20-to-1 level. For every negative interaction, family members have at least 10 positive ones. As one father told us, "You pay a big price when you verbally attack your loved ones. You hurt them deeply, and they don't forget quickly. I always feel like I need to pay a bit of penance after attacking them and try very hard to focus on their strengths as much as possible."

John DeFrain once gave a homework assignment in a college class on parenting he was teaching. Students were encouraged to tell their parents about the good feelings they had for them. This never happens in many families, and it can be quite difficult for family members to be more verbal about their deepest emotions. "I can't do that," one 6-foot-6 farm boy complained to the professor. "Do it or you'll flunk the assignment," the professor teased the student with a smile.

The next week the young man came back to class. "How'd it go?" the professor asked. "I couldn't do it," he replied, looking down at his shoes. "Do it!" the professor urged.

The next week the young man came back to class, this time with a big smile on his face. "What happened?" one of the other students asked.

"Dad and I were working on the tractor stuck in the mud out in the field. We were in our overalls, covered with mud. I said to him, 'Dad …' He looked at me kind of funny.

"I said, 'Dad, I love you,' and I threw my arms around him. And he stood there like a stunned rock for a second and then he hugged me back and said, 'I love you, Son,' and we stood there together in the mud, patting each other on the back and hugging each other and crying. It felt so good."

Express the strong, positive feelings you have for each other in your family, and the feelings will grow.

How to Be Nice

What makes a stable marriage? Many researchers in the United States and around the world have focused on that question. John Gottmann, a psychology professor, and his colleagues at the University of Washington have conducted scientific experiments for 20 years with more than 2,000 couples. The research team observed couples interacting with each other in a campus "marriage laboratory," using video cameras, EKG monitors and specially-designed instruments.

The investigators looked at how couples talk to each other. They examined facial expressions, gestures, fidgeting behaviors, and so forth, as well as physiological clues including changes in heartbeat and breathing during disagreements.

What separated those couples who stayed together after the conclusion of the laboratory research from those who divorced within the next couple years? We love Gottmann's answer: The couples in stable marriages were simply "nicer to each other."

Gottmann himself had to chuckle at the simplicity of the answer to the question that researchers pose. This answer reflects our own understanding of successful marriages and families, also gained through many years of study and reflection.

But if being nice to each other and loving one another were all that easy, people wouldn't have as much trouble creating strong marriages and families as they seem to be having now. What, then, can be done in our efforts to love each other?

High on our list is the importance of keeping our interactions positive. Negative energy—such a common element of human relationships—is destructive and demoralizing. It hurts us, takes away our confidence and self-esteem, and distances us from each other.

When we're upset about something, which is inevitable in life, the path of least resistance is to get angry and lash out at other people. Loved ones, amazingly, take the brunt of all this anger because if we were to act this way at work or school, we would soon be shown the door.

Under stress we regress, as the saying goes. We regress to the vicious and foolish behavior we learned on the playground, among other places, when we were young children. For many of us, it is probably important to admit that when we see adults act in ways that would make a well-behaved 7-year-old shudder, it does hold a certain fascination. Right? At first, we are fascinated. Then, revulsion and embarrassment set in, for we see the person is falling into the same trap we can so easily fall into. The old childhood tapes are still readily accessed, and we can play them with ease. A good tantrum makes us feel important and self-righteous—for a while.

But soon after, the feelings of shame and foolishness set in. We know we have failed to do what is best. And what, again, is that?

Search carefully for positive ways to interact with each other. This includes positive talk and positive actions. In the world of words, there is always a way to say precisely what we want to say, and to say it in a positive manner. In the world of actions, there is always a way to behave with grace, dignity and kindness.

This is not the easiest path, by any means. It takes more time to use our brain and create new ways of talking with each other, more time and thought than it takes to simply bark. But we can do it. No matter what happens, no matter how difficult the situation, we can find a positive way to respond. In both the short and long run, this will be better for our relationships with each other.

Showing Appreciation and Affection

For some reason, many of us got it planted in our heads that to express appreciation is an act of weakness or an act that will somehow poison the "victim" of one's praise. "She knows how important she is to me," is commonly said, "and I really don't need to tell her." In the case of our children, we sometimes harbor the vague and contorted belief that if we were to actually thank them for being who they are and hazard verbal and/or physical affection, it would somehow swell their heads.

But if too much praise swells the head, does too little praise cause one's head to shrivel up or implode?

For a number of years we conducted a series of relationship enrichment workshops for couples. We experimented with various ways of helping people practice expressing appreciation and affection. We invited couples who were doing pretty well in their relationship and who wanted to enhance the good feelings they already had for each other.

We asked each individual to write down all the reasons they had for loving their partner. We gave them plenty of time to do this and then asked the couples to come to the front of the room to share what they had to say before the group. We knew this would be difficult for people, especially in front of others. But we felt it was important to do for at least three reasons: so we could all get a better understanding of why human beings love each other; so we could get some good practice sharing these feelings; and so we could triple underline the importance of these feelings by sharing them with others. In human cultures, weddings are public events because they signify the sanctity of human connection for all who attend. A relationship enhancement workshop was another way of blessing humans' love for each other.

The first woman who volunteered to talk had a long list for her partner. Here are some of her reasons:

"I love you, Bill, because you're such a good listener. You let me talk about my day and what's important in my life, and you clearly enjoy what I have to say.

"I love you because you're funny. You have such a great sense of humor.

"You're very honest with me and everyone else in your life, and I think this is very, very important. But you're honest in a gentle way.

"I love you because you're so patient and kind to the kids. You hardly ever get mad, and when you do, you have pretty much every reason to do so.

"I'm proud of you for what you do in your profession. You are so good at your work, and you make enough money to make a good life possible for all of us.

"You're handy around the house, and that saves us a lot of money.

"I love you because I know you love me.

"Oh, and I love you because you're a great lover!"

It was an extraordinarily moving moment for all of us in the room. Bill, of course, was almost overwhelmed with feeling. "Oh, gosh," he breathed. "I don't know what to say." He was next, however, and he did an excellent job of telling the good things he admired about his partner Allison. The hushed group witnessing this very intimate moment in life was captivated.

To emphasize the importance of these events, we videotaped each interchange. We played them all back, especially so each couple could see themselves: There was Joe reading his list and saying, off-handedly, "Oh, Sue knows all this," while Susan's eyes glistened in appreciation for getting the chance to hear it all once again. And there was Alexander, always stoic, listening so intently to Maria, trying to swallow his emotions.

We had homework in class and the assignment after this session was to take these wonderful expressions of love and do something special with them. "Write them down in a card for your partner, have them framed, put them in the beginning pages of a book of poetry, create a refrigerator magnet, whatever you would like," the assignment read. "Make them a permanent expression of how you feel about each other."

Three weeks later Maria came up before the evening's discussion began and displayed a beautiful locket on a gold chain she had around her neck. "Inside is a tiny scroll," she beamed. "Alexander had the reasons he loves me inscribed by a calligrapher in tiny letters on a scroll tied by a small ribbon. It's wonderful!"

Teaching and Learning About Appreciation and Affection

Showing appreciation for each other in the family doesn't have to be something elaborate, but it is important that it be done regularly—so often that it becomes a habit. For kids, a hug, a kiss on the cheek, a little tussling and playfulness—all of these work great, especially when they're little.

As they grow older they start wanting to hide their emotions as a protective device and to appear more grown up, so they may be less defensive sometimes when we write them a nice, simple note—even a sticky-note placed strategically here and there in the kitchen or their room, thanking them for being who they are. We don't want to let them get too grown up too fast, so the little kid things still work occasionally: when we're 14 we still have some 4-year-old in us. In fact, when we're 35 or 55 we still have some 4-year-old in us, thank goodness.

Simply "hanging out" with your children, as young people say, is a show of appreciation and affection. In the adolescent years they often want to spend lots of time with their friends, but think creatively about what they like to do and where they like to go so you can figure out ways to be with them and show them, nonverbally, how much you enjoy their company and, thus, how much you like them.

A long car ride together is a wonderful place to talk in relative peace—both parent and adolescent are captive audiences to each other. The phone is not ringing (if you turn the demanding cell phone off!), the TV isn't yammering, and you have the wonderful and rare opportunity of simply focusing on each other. In a conversation with a young person, the best way to show appreciation is to listen to them. Don't lecture them, don't reprimand them, simply listen and show how much you respect them and value their views of the world.

In the adolescent years it's sometimes easy to fall into the trap of distancing from our children as they distance from us as parents, and then we as parents come to the conclusion that the young people don't want to be around us, and the young people come to a similar wrong conclusion that we don't want to be with them. We mirror acceptance and appreciation toward each other, reflecting positive images back and forth in our reactions to each other's facial expressions.

Likewise, we mirror negativity. When an adolescent looks grumpy or distant or preoccupied, for whatever reason, we tend to take it too personally and respond with a grumpy, negative, put-upon demeanor, also. This is a dangerous, chronic trap we all can fall into. We can end up reading more negativity into the relationship than there really is, and we can end up compounding the problem so it becomes a self-fulfilling prophecy pushing us apart. As parents we need to think about ways to avoid these pitfalls, and to do this takes a great deal of creativity and careful communication.

Finally, as adults we need to be continually conscious of the fact that we are teachers. We teach our children appreciation and affection, commitment, and all the other wonderful qualities of strong families. We need to begin this education process very early so positive behavior in the family and with others in the community becomes habitual with children from a young age onward. This doesn't happen by stern lecturing or reprimanding the young. It happens by teaching them in very loving ways how to appreciate each other and express love. We can't make them do good things when we're concentrating on making them feel bad.

Instead, we say, "Thank you, Ellie!" We smile to our toddler, as she gives us her ball to play with. And we turn this into a game: "And here, Ellie, I'm rolling your ball back to you. Can you say 'Thank you, Daddy?'" Back and forth, back and forth: "Thank you, Daddy!" and "Thank you, Ellie!" It turns into a pleasing game for parent and child. Just as we learn how to play sports, prepare nutritious meals, paint pictures and fix cars, we learn to show appreciation and affection for each other in our families through conscious efforts at teaching and learning. This is done in a warm, connecting spirit, and it needs to begin early.

Strengths-based Activities for Enhancing Appreciation and Affection in the Family

Acts of Kindness

Objective:

To encourage family members to show others in the family that they are appreciated or valued. Kindness does not have to cost money. It can just be showing thoughtfulness and consideration. Make kindness a habit.

Supplies Needed:

Paper and pencil for drawing names. (No other supplies needed unless a particular act of kindness requires additional supplies.)

Step-by-Step Instructions:

1. Talk about ways to show others that they are special or that you appreciate or value them. (Examples: Make their favorite food for supper, give a hug, do one of their chores, make their bed, say "hello" or "good morning" to them/ "please" and "thank you", etc.)

2. Put each person's name on a piece of paper and put them all in a bowl.

3. Have each family member draw another family member's name from the bowl. Sometime during the specified day or week, each family member should do at least one act of kindness for the family member they have drawn. An example could be to help them with or do a chore for them. Spend some extra time with them doing something they want to do.

Discussion Questions:

1. How did you feel when you performed an act of kindness for someone else?

2. What was the hardest part about doing the act?

3. How does it make you feel to know that someone is trying to do special things for you?

4. Share how it felt to have an act of kindness done for you.

5. What is the best thing that someone could do to make you feel special or appreciated?

6. What acts of kindness might you be willing to do on a regular basis for family members, extended family, neighbors, friends, other people you know at work and school?

7. How might this make the world a better place to live in?

Board of Directors

Objective:

To think about people who have been influential in your life and how you can be influential in the lives of others.

Supplies Needed:

Blank paper and pencil for each person.

Step-by-Step Instructions:

1. Imagine that you are seated in a company's board of directors' meeting room. Draw a large oval to represent the table in the center of the room. Make X's spaced around the table to represent chairs for the board of directors.

2. Think of the people who have had a positive influence on you during your lifetime. Put one person's name on each of the X's. This might be parents, grandparents, aunts or uncles, teachers, neighbors—anyone who has had a positive impact on you.

3. Next to each name put one or two words that describe the impact that person has had on you, e.g., encouragement, unconditional love, teaching, etc.

Discussion Questions:

1. Who has been the most influential person in your life?

2. What is one specific thing that person has done to be so influential?

3. How can you live your life so the people you know will want to put you on their board of directors?

How Well Do You Know Your Family?

Objective:

For parents and adolescent children to be able to see the world through the eyes of each other. Knowing and wanting to find out about someone shows that you truly care. What's more, it can be fun!

Supplies Needed:

Pen/pencil and copies of the parent and child question pages.

Step-by-Step Instructions:

1. Grab a pencil! Have your son/daughter try to answer the questions about you, their parent(s).

2. At the same time, the parent(s) should answer the sheet of questions about their son/daughter.

3. When all are finished, exchange and correct one another's worksheets. Discuss each other's answers together.

Discussion Questions:

1. Were these questions hard/easy to answer?

2. What did you learn that you did not previously know? Why?

3. What surprised you about the right answers?

4. What feelings do you have now that you know the answers?

How Well Do You Know Your Parents?

(Note: Please adapt these questions to the person(s) you are living with or answering the questions with.)

1. How did your parents meet?

2. What color are the eyes of your parent(s)?

3. If your parent(s) went on a trip to a foreign city, would she/he head first to a historic site or a museum, the shopping streets or a café?

4. For a vacation, would your parent(s) prefer a luxury resort, a rustic mountain cabin, or resting at home?

5. What presidential candidate did your parent(s) vote for in the last election?

6. Does your parent(s) believe in love at first sight?

7. For a pleasant evening, would your parent(s) rather watch TV with the family, sit alone and read, or go to dinner with friends?

8. Does your parent(s) gas up the car as soon as the tank is half empty or when the fuel is nearly gone?

9. Does your parent(s) usually carry a photo of you in her/his wallet?

10. How old was your parent(s) on his/her first date?

11. If your parent(s) turned on the TV and found these choices, which would he/she pick: a football game, soap opera, old movie—or turn off the television?

12. Which of these can't your parent(s) do: touch her/his toes, do a headstand, rewire a lamp, replace the spark plugs, sew a shirt?

13. Which of these can't your parent(s) do: a somersault, make a basketball free throw, prepare a meal, change a flat tire, sew on a button?

14. What was the first full-time job of your parent(s)?

15. Who is the closest friend of your parent(s)?

16. What gift would your parent(s) most like to receive?

17. If your parent(s) could have you do anything for three hours, what would it be?

Tally Up:

More than 15 right answers: Congratulations—you really know your parents.
11 to 15 right: Not bad, but try to pay a little more attention.
Fewer than 11 right: You need a crash course called "Parents 101."

How Well Do You Know Your Child?

1. What is your daughter's/son's favorite game or sport?

2. What embarrasses your daughter/son the most?

3. Who is your daughter's/son's closest friend?

4. If your daughter/son could do anything she/he chose for a day, what would it be?

5. What is your daughter's/son's favorite color?

6. What was the last movie your daughter/son saw?

7. What is your daughter's/son's favorite thing to do after school?

8. Which is your daughter's/son's favorite dinner: steak/salad, hamburger/fries, chicken/corn?

9. What has been the biggest disappointment in your daughter's/son's life this year?

10. Who is your daughter's/son's favorite singer or musical group?

11. If your daughter/son had a choice to buy a pet, what would it be?

12. Which would your daughter/son rather do: wash dishes, mow the lawn, clean her/his room, or vacuum the house?

13. Do your daughter's/son's friends call her/him by a nickname? If so, what is it?

14. What really makes your daughter/son angry?

15. What was the last problem your daughter/son came to you for help with?

16. What gift would your daughter/son most like to receive?

17. What does your daughter/son do that he/she is proud of?

Tally up:

More than 15 right answers: Congratulations—you really know your daughter/son.

11 to 15 right: Not bad, but try to pay a little more attention.

Fewer than 11 right: Better spend a little more time catching up on what's new with your child.

Family Memories Book

Objective:

To have fun together and make a family memories book.

Supplies Needed:

8 ½-by-11-inch paper, color or black and white pictures of family members, pencils or pens, glue stick or double-sided tape, notebook or photo album and stickers (optional).

Step-by-Step Instructions:

1. Make a family album including an assortment of pictures of family members and activities (photographs or drawings), programs from school or church activities, special stories written by family members, greeting cards, and anything else with special meaning to family members.

2. Family members can label each item and add comments about each occasion. (For families experiencing divorce, a family album can be created for the child who will be living in a different place.)

3. Every family member should write a couple of lines about the items on the page. Remember to have at least one item from each family member. Stickers can be used to decorate the pages. Themes for pages might be: holiday gatherings, family vacations, summertime outings, family picnics, school days, family pets, etc.

4. Arrange the pages in a notebook or photo album.

5. As new pages are created, they can be added to the family memories book. Families can bring the album out every month or two to add a new page or look at past events.

Discussion Questions:

1. What is your favorite family memory?

2. What other memories did the pictures bring to mind?

3. What makes an event stick in your mind so that it becomes a favorite memory?

4. Can you think of some other themes for creating additional memory pages?

5. Why is it fun to have an album to look at?

6. What do you remember about this page when you made it?

7. How have family members changed in appearance over time?

I Appreciate My Family

Objective:

All family members will gain a better idea of how they can appreciate one another and show signs of appreciation.

Supplies Needed:

Paper and pencils.

Step-by-Step Instructions:

1. Draw a picture of your family. Briefly label each family member's role in your life.

2. As a family, discuss the following questions: What do you appreciate most about each of your family members? What do you think they appreciate most about you?

3. Appreciation and affection can be shown in many different ways. Write down the name of the family member you think would like to be shown each of the methods of appreciation in the boxes below. List other ways to show appreciation and affection and match those to your family members.

Method of Appreciation	Who in My Family Would Like It?	Other Ways to Show I Appreciate Them
Write her/him a poem		
Do an art project with her/him		
Make her/him a handmade card		
Make her/him a handmade gift		
Make her/him a special food		
Sing her or his favorite song		

Discussion Questions:

1. What did you learn about your family from this activity?

2. What are two of the things from the list you will do to show your family members you appreciate them?

3. How would you like other family members to show they appreciate you?

Family Strengths Bingo

Objective:

To learn new things about your family and identify some of the strengths your family has.

Supplies Needed:

Family Strengths Bingo Cards, pencils, 25 beans or substitute objects for each player, master calling sheet and slips of paper numbered 1 to 50.

Step-by-Step Instructions:

1. Pass out a Bingo card (page 31), 25 beans and a pencil to each player.

2. Have each player write a number from 1 to 10 at random in the corner box for each of the five squares in the column under the letter "B". Use each number only one time. Under the letter "I", put random numbers from 11 to 20 in the corner. Again use each number only one time. Continue with the numbers for the columns under the letters "N" (21-30), "G" (31-40), and "O" (41-50).

3. In a container have papers numbered from 1 to 50 with the appropriate letter included. Call out a number and place on a Bingo calling sheet.

4. Have participants start by placing a bean in the FREE SPACE. Participants who are able to place a bean on a square need to read what is in that square and then do or tell what it states.

5. The first person to get 5 in a row horizontally, vertically or diagonally shouts BINGO. To play longer, you can do a cross, a plus sign or a blackout.

Discussion Questions:

1. What did you learn new about your family members?

2. Which one of the squares that you covered was the easiest to do? Why?

3. Which was the hardest to do? Why?

4. As you look at your family, what are some of the strengths your family has?

Family Strengths

B 1-10	I 11-20	N 21-30	G 31-40	O 41-50
Name a fun family activity you all do together.	Give a compliment to each family member.	Share something you would like to do as a family but haven't.	Share a happy event in your life.	Say something positive to each family member.
Stand up and let everyone give you applause.	If you could change places with one family member for a day, who would it be and why?	What is one of your favorite family traditions?	Share what you consider to be a personal accomplishment.	Give someone in your family a hug.
Name something funny that has happened in your family.	Share one thing about a family ancestor.	FREE SPACE	What community service activity does your family do?	Share the greatest compliment that you have received.
Give a compliment to the second person on your right.	Describe something someone could do to make you happy.	Say something positive about yourself.	What do you think makes your family a happy family?	What is your favorite childhood memory?
Describe what you would consider a "perfect family vacation."	Would family members say you are more like a kitten or a tiger? Why?	Share what makes your family special.	Talk about three things you are grateful for.	Tell the first person on your left one thing you really like about her/him.

Family Welcome Quilt or Recipe Book

Objective:

To welcome a new family member to the family or give a memorable gift to new-lyweds.

Supplies Needed:

For the quilt you will need fabric for quilt blocks, embroidery floss, fabric paints, crayons or pens and a sewing machine. For the recipe book you will need pens, pencils, crayons, a three-ring binder and binder paper of predetermined size.

Step-by-Step Instructions:

Family Welcome Quilt

1. Give each family member a quilt block and floss with instructions for the colors to embroider.

2. After blocks are completed, plan a time when the family can get together to assemble the blocks and quilt the quilt by hand or using a sewing machine. (If this is not something the family can do, hire a quilter to do the quilting.) This is an activity that will let you enjoy time together as a family and the recipient(s) will receive a very unique gift.

Recipe Book

1. Ask family members to contribute their favorite recipes.

2. Put the recipes on a predetermined size of paper, sorted according to categories (such as main dishes, vegetables, salads and desserts), and compile in a book. A three-ring binder could be used to make the book.

3. Younger family members could make pictures for each of the category dividers and make a cover. Family members all have a chance to contribute and the recipient(s) receives a very unique gift.

Discussion Questions:

1. What talents is your family willing to share with new family members?

2.   What other hobbies does your family share?

3.   For what other occasions might the quilt or recipe book be appropriate? (anniversaries, religious events, graduations, etc.)

4.   What did you learn about your family as you did this project?

Group Affirmation

Objective:

To affirm and encourage each family member.

Supplies Needed:

Paper and pencils.

Step-by-Step Instructions:

1.   Select one family member and write her/his name at the top of a piece of paper. (This might be done on a person's birthday, or just take turns doing it for each family member.)

2.   Pass the paper around the entire family and have each person write, "This is what I've learned to appreciate about you," or "This is what I like about you," followed by something specific that they like or appreciate about the person. Only a phrase or one sentence is needed.

3.   When the sheet has been passed to everyone, give it to the person whose name is on the top.

Discussion Questions:

1.   How difficult was it to write what you liked or appreciated about the family member you selected?

2.   Why is it sometimes easier to criticize and complain than to build up and encourage?

3.   How can your family make showing appreciation and affection more a part of your family's daily life?

4. Additional question for the person who received the sheet about herself/himself: How did it feel to hear all these good things from other family members?

Family Place Mats

Objective:

We are all special in many ways and have many talents. Children need to be reminded that they are unique in many ways. Making and using special place mats will remind each person of their talents and special character traits.

Supplies Needed:

A 14-inch by 22-inch piece of poster board (half a standard poster board) for each person, colored markers, colored pencils and crayons, scissors, magazines and newspapers that show pictures of activities or interests that your kids have, any personal items that your children have that show their interests, clear contact paper or access to a laminating machine, glue.

Step-by-Step Instructions:

1. Each family member will be making a place mat for mealtimes. Both sides of the place mats will be decorated with a collage. One side will represent "These are the things I like." Pictures from magazines, letters from magazine headlines made into words, drawings and sayings can be put on this side of the mat.

2. The other side of the mat will represent "What makes me who I am." This side also will be decorated with a collage using the same techniques. On this side of the place mat, the collage will represent characteristics of the person, such as funny, happy, caring, smart, good at music, a good listener.

3. After both sides are decorated, the place mat needs to be covered with clear contact paper or laminated.

4. Use the place mats at least once a week. Talk about what is on the place mats.

5. Have family members make a new place mat each year and see how they change. As you use them over the years, you can talk about the "good old

days." Wouldn't the grandchildren love to see what their mom and dad were like when they were their age?

Discussion Questions:

1.   How hard was it to get things that represent you?

2.   What are some of your best traits on your place mat?

3.   How does each place mat differ from each other in likes and dislikes?

4.   Share some of your good traits with family members.

Commitment to Each Other

Before reading the next section, take a few minutes to see how you think you're doing on commitment as a family and/or couple. Fill out the assessment on the next page. You can then discuss your responses to the items, and talk about the strengths you demonstrate with each other and the areas of potential growth you would like to enhance. A planning guide is included so you can develop some goals. You might think about which of the activities at the end of this unit you want to complete for increasing your commitment to your family and to your mate. Some are geared toward your family; others are specifically for couples. Most of the activities can be adjusted to meet the needs of your family, whatever its composition. Be creative and good luck!

American Family Strengths Inventory©

Commitment to Each Other

Family members can record their perceptions here in the area of *Commitment to Each Other*. Feel free to make copies of this page for each member of your family, or get additional copies of this Inventory in the Appendix. Once each member has completed the Inventory, record their responses on the Tally Sheet provided in the Appendix.

You may want to complete this survey now, then again in three months and again in another six months. That way, you can see how your family is progressing.

Put an "S" for Strength beside the qualities you feel your family has achieved and a "G" beside those qualities that are an area of potential Growth. If the particular characteristic does not apply to your family or is not a characteristic that is important to you, put an "NA" for Not Applicable. After recording your perceptions, spend some enjoyable time talking together about how your views are similar and how they are different. Remember: No one is absolutely right and no one is absolutely wrong on this. Everyone has a valid perception of what is happening, and everyone's views need to be considered carefully and respectfully. If you see ways to work together to enhance your strengths in the area of *Commitment to Each Other*, feel free to jump in and do so in the coming days and weeks.

Family Member's Name:_____ Date:_____

In Our Family ...

Responsibilities are shared fairly.   _____

Everyone gets a say in making decisions.   _____

Individuals are allowed to make their own choices and encouraged to
take responsibility for these choices.   _____

We find it easy to trust each other.   _____

We like to do things for each other that make us feel good about
ourselves.   _____

We have reasonable expectations for each other.   _____

We allow each other to be ourselves.   _____

We have a high regard for each other.   _____

We respect the roles each of us plays in the family.   _____

We find it easy to be honest with each other.   _____

We accept that each of us has different ways of doing things.   _____

We build each other's self-esteem.   _____

All things considered, we value each other and are committed to our well-being as a family.   _____

© Copyrighted material. For nonprofit educational purposes only. Not for resale.

Our Plan for Commitment to Each Other

Now that you know your family's strengths related to commitment to each other, read the next section. As you read, you may want to think about how the examples fit your family. You can then look at ways your family might strengthen their commitment to each other and write them in the space below. The activities at the end of this section are there to help you get started.

Our Plan

Based on our discussion about Commitment to Each Other, *we have decided to do the following things in the coming weeks and months to demonstrate how we value each other and are committed to each other's well-being.*

1. _____

_____

_____

_____

2. _____

_____

_____

_____

3. _____

_____

_____

_____

Signed: _____   _____

_____   _____

_____   _____

The Family Comes First

While doing our recent research on strong families in Australia, we heard story after story of the incredible staying power that family members demonstrate toward each other. "What are the qualities that make you a strong family?" we would ask. The person responding would often look down in deep thought, rub his hands as the search continued for the precise answer, and then finally throw up his hands in dismay: "We're ... just ... there for each other!" would fly out on a wave of emotion.

Words don't really describe this phenomenon very well, but the emotions attached to the words conveyed the message quite clearly. Strong families are committed to each other above all else. The family comes first.

Let us qualify that a bit. In some families who speak in traditionally religious terms, God is first. The life of the family is dedicated to God and the members' connection to the greater good in the world. But it becomes very clear when continuing the discussions with these families that God and family are intimately linked in their minds, and one can express a love for God through loving one's family.

Let's listen to the family members themselves:

> My wife bought me an expensive wedding ring for our first anniversary. This symbolized to me that she thought we were going to be together for a long time.

> —

> We give each other the freedom and encouragement to pursue individual goals. Yet both of us would cut out activities or goals that threaten our existence as a couple. She has a wonderful job that she loves, but she wouldn't transfer to another city if I couldn't go happily, and vice versa.

> —

> As I think back over the years, I bet my wife and I have attended literally hundreds of school meetings, school plays, sports events, church events, clubs, you-name-it ... all focusing on our children's activities outside the home. Our children when they were growing up were all smart, energetic, active kids and loved being involved in things, and add all these activities to the normal school conferences and lunches and meetings and it got pretty challenging at times to keep up. I do admit to thinking to myself, with a smile: "Wow! Only three more teacher conference afternoons like this and we'll have all the kids out of high school and I can relax some!" Fortunately, through the years I kept

focused on the reality of the situation: Our dedication to the kids and their activities was an investment in the well-being of our whole family and it was well worth the effort. We needed to be there to support them and show we would always be around and on their side and committed to their growth. And today, they're wonderful adults with neat kids of their own.

—

Divorce is not an option for us. We do fight; sometimes we don't sleep in the same bed. There's nothing wrong with sleeping apart. You find out how cold your bed can be without your partner.

—

My husband and I decided that family is very important to us. Our relationship and our relationship with our children will outlast jobs and cars and houses. We have a goal of making our family healthy and loving; we work at it.

—

When my husband and I split up four years ago, I thought, "Well, there goes my dream of Mom, Dad and the kids. There goes any hope I ever had of having a family." But we have adjusted to the situation—the kids pitch in and help in many, many ways, and Grandma and Grandpa are with us all the way. We've created a new family for ourselves and the foundation is built on the fact that we will always be here for each other. That feels good.

Besides valuing the family as a unit, strong families do not lose sight of the value of each individual family member. Each person forms a part of the family and each part is precious.

Commitment includes sexual fidelity. Some of the couples in the research noted that there had been a crisis earlier in the relationship when an extramarital affair had come to light. Some marriages end at this point, and for other marriages this can signal a new beginning in which the couple does some serious talking with each other and creates a sound foundation for continuing on together. Commitment describes a special kind of love we have for each other—a love that is steady and sure and is not subject to mood swings, the passage of the years, or hard times. It is commitment that endures.

In families, commitment means slowing down in life and treating each other with respect. It means making our children our priority in life. As one father said to us:

> When the kids ask me to do something with them, I always try to say yes right away. I know if I keep putting them off, eventually they will stop asking. They will learn that their father doesn't really care about them, he cares more about mowing the lawn and washing the car. And, if I couldn't say yes right away, I'd ask for a minute, two minutes, no more than five minutes to finish what I was doing. To a young child, even five minutes is a long time, and I didn't want to lose that golden opportunity to be a Dad.

We teach commitment to our children by modeling commitment ourselves, by putting family first and demonstrating by our behavior that we love to do things with them and be with them and this is a fact they can count on. As they grow older and become more verbal, we can talk with them about commitment and keeping promises. Their lives are full of situations in which they have to balance competing interests:

- "Should I go here with Bill or there with Randy?"

- "I promised Joey I'd come over to his house, but now I've got this great chance to go bike-riding with the team."

- "I don't want to go with the family! I want to be with my friends!"

Our children's dilemmas in life are just as challenging to them as the dilemmas that we face as adults. When they run into these inevitable dilemmas, they are at teachable moments: times we can demonstrate our own commitment to them by sitting down and talking with them about how they can honor their own commitments in life and show the respect to their family members and friends that all deserve. Family especially.

Sometimes these discussions will not be easy ones, but we cannot afford to let our children grow up without understanding the importance of commitment, for it is a foundation element of strong marital and family relationships.

I Should Have Spent More Time at Work

"When you're sick in the hospital and think you're dying of cancer, it isn't the boss who comes and holds your hand."

That's one form of a common epiphany many people experience in life: a flash of insight when it becomes painfully clear that the values so desperately driving us are questionable.

National surveys consistently report that Americans as a group value family first, work second. Whether this professed commitment to the family is consistently demonstrated in actual behavior at home is another question altogether.

In a society that elevates competition to a spiritual level, we often focus on our work life to the detriment of our home life. Of course, this is often hard to admit. One very busy judge had his morning of epiphany before the bathroom mirror while shaving: "I always told my wife and kids that I was working so hard for them. The long hours were for *their* benefit. But that morning in the mirror I finally admitted it. 'Bull!' I said to the mirror. 'Quit lying to everyone. You're doing it for *you*. Not them.'" This burst of honesty became the impetus for setting limits on his work life and he began building meaningful connections with his family.

Women fall into the same trap. Sometimes they do this by re-creating the workaholic approach to life that men seem to have pioneered. Sometimes wives strike a silent bargain with their husbands that trades emotional connection for financial security.

Financial security has always been high on the list of reasons people, especially women, have for choosing a particular partner. Even men have been known to chuckle, "It's as easy to marry a rich one as a poor one." But today we have added friendship to the equation. As a culture we value emotional commitment between spouses, and so the need for a better balance between work and home is ever-present. The marriage satisfaction bar has, in essence, been raised considerably.

The key for family members is finding a level of commitment and emotional bond that works for everyone. Each of us has different needs in this regard, and some compromises often need to be worked out. For what it's worth, we vote for a commitment to family over work, and making this commitment long before it's too late. An ounce of prevention is worth a ton of cure when it comes to family dynamics.

When people in the news step down from a high-powered job, they almost always say, with a bit of humility, perhaps shame, "I'm going to spend more time with my family." And, we have yet to hear a story of someone saying, at the end of life, "I should have spent more time at work."

Strengths-based Activities for Enhancing Commitment to Each Other

Family Folklore

Objectives:

To learn about your own family history; to learn some of the events and experiences that make your family unique; to build a sense of connection across family generations.

Supplies Needed:

Paper and pencil. A tape recorder or video camera would also be useful.

Step-by-Step Instructions:

1. Suggest that your child/children interview you or other relatives about family memories they have.

2. Make up a list of questions ahead of time. Here are some questions to start with:

    •   What region(s) or country(ies) did our family come from?

    •   Do we celebrate special occasions like birthdays, weddings and holidays the same way our ancestors used to celebrate them?

    •   How did you celebrate holidays when you were young?

    •   What special games or food do you remember?

    •   What dances, songs or languages do you know from the "old days"? Who could teach us the "old days" dances, songs or languages?

    •   Who in the family has any costumes, toys, crafts or recipes from our family's past?

    •   Who in the family could teach us to make our family traditional foods or crafts?

3. Decide on a way to keep the stories together and pass them on to others in the family, both for current and future generations.

Discussion Questions:

1. What was the most interesting thing you learned?

2. What surprised you most about your family's past?

3. How does your family history influence the way your family is today?

4. What special things can you do to make a difference in your family's future history?

Your, My and Our Traditions

Objective:

To strengthen family bonds by creating and practicing family traditions.

Supplies Needed:

None.

Step-by-Step instructions:

1. Every family of origin has traditions. As new families are formed, it is important to talk about each person's traditions.

2. Discuss these questions: Which traditions do you want to retain? Which traditions are OK to drop? What new traditions would you like to create?

3. Think about each holiday or special event and talk to the family about what makes this celebration special to your family. These are the things that kids will remember and pass on to their children when they become adults. Here are a few ideas, "When our family leaves on vacation, we always leave at 6:00 in the morning!" "We always have turkey for Thanksgiving and ham for Christmas." "Whoever had a birthday got to eat from the red plate." "After getting shots at the doctor, we got to get an ice cream cone on the way home." "In our family we played cards after every family meal."

Discussion Questions:

1. What family traditions do you have?

2.   If you are in a blended family, how have you incorporated traditions from both families? Made new ones?

3.   How do traditions give you a sense of belonging to your family?

4.   Which family traditions were you surprised to learn were important to different family members?

Filling the Cookie Jar

Objective:

To remember a family member who is far away.

Supplies Needed:

Stationery and pen/pencil, or computer, cookie jar.

Step-by-Step Instructions:

1.   As a family, think of a grandparent or another relative you don't see very often.

2.   Make paper cookies that you can use to fill the cookie jar.

3.   Have each family member write some "remember whens" or draw some pictures if the children are very small.

4.   Put all the paper cookies in the cookie jar.

5.   On the outside of the cookie jar put a tag that says something like this: "Dear _____. While we were growing up you always had homemade treats for us, usually cookies. Inside this cookie jar are our treats to you. You provided us with many memories and we have written them down for you to read when you have a quiet minute from time to time over the year. It is our way of letting you know how often we think of you even though many miles separate us." OR "You always had a full cookie jar. Since we are not together as much, here is a full cookie jar of memories that you can enjoy all year long."

Discussion Questions:

1. Why is it important to keep in touch with relatives that you do not see as often?

2. How can the feeling of *family* be promoted or nurtured even when we are far away?

3. What other ways can we use to keep our family connected even though we live far apart?

Hand Prints

Objective:

To keep track of a child's growth and remind your child of your ongoing commitment to her/him.

Supplies Needed:

Select the items appropriate for the activity you choose: plain paper, fabric apron/quilt blocks, stepping stone with fast-setting concrete, fabric paint, tempera paint.

Step-by-Step Instructions:

This activity won't slow down the hands of time, but it will give you and your child/children a tangible record of her/his growth.

The idea is to make hand prints of each child periodically to see how much they have grown. You can decide together how often to do this. Perhaps you'll want to do it each New Year's Day, on the first day of the month of their birthday, or the first day of every month!

1. Lay out a piece of plain paper.

2. Put a small amount of tempera paint in a foil pie plate or a large plastic lid.

3. Have your child lay her or his hand flat in the tempera paint, then press it onto the paper. Press gently on each finger to make a complete print.

4. Allow the paint to dry. Then date the hand print. Your child may want to sign it or add appropriate notes about what else of importance was happening at the time the hand print was made.

5. Keep hand prints in a special envelope or bind them together in a booklet. Compare the new print with past prints each time to note how much your child has grown. (Make the hand print a different color each time for added variety.)

6. The promise of making hand prints together at predetermined times can remind your child of your ongoing commitment to her or him.

Variations:

1. At a big extended family gathering, have each member make a hand print on a quilt block with fabric paint. Let family members arrange blocks in a pattern. Sew blocks together if you can or find someone else to do it for you. The next time the extended family is together, members could tie the quilt. Decide how the quilt will be displayed. If you wish, make sufficient quilt blocks so that each nuclear family can have its own quilt, also.

2. Make stepping stones out of the hand prints. Use fast-setting concrete and a disposable form to make the print.

3. Have young children put hand prints on an apron to give as a gift to another family member.

Discussion Questions:

1. What new things have you learned since we made our last hand prints?

2. What plans do you have to continue your family record?

3. How has your family changed since the creation of the family quilt or last family record?

4. What things are different about the family members since they made the last hand print?

Harvesting Our Heritage

Objective:

To preserve and/or create favorite family recipes, cooking traditions and the fond memories surrounding them.

Supplies Needed:

Some sort of scrapbook—to be created as a family. Materials needed for the book will depend on personal preferences and individual creativity. Heritage books can be store-bought scrapbooks that have been personalized with special decorations or covers, or handmade binders of wood, cardboard or plastic. Other materials could include photos, recipe cards, paper, pencils, markers, crayons, paints, stickers, beads, ribbon, glue, tape, scissors, etc.

Step-by-Step Instructions:

1. Ask family members to contribute their favorite recipes from their childhood, including special memories surrounding the food, the occasion or the tradition.

2. Children can "interview" grandparents, aunts, uncles and cousins to find out what kinds of foods were important "back then."

3. Encourage them to ask questions about the food—why it was memorable, how it made them feel, etc. Find out if there are pictures—perhaps Grandpa carving the turkey or making his special "Cranberry Walnut Stuffing" that the family has raved about all these years.

4. The family creates a book to store the gathered information with each contributing to the decoration and design. More recipes and traditions can be added through time.

Variations:

1. Plan a family meal using old family recipes.

2. Use technology (make video/audio recording or DVD) to record family heritage interviews.

3. Ask parents/grandparents about their favorite childhood memories.

4. Convert old family movies to current technology.

5. Convert old family photos to DVD or video.

6. Create a family photo album.

Discussion Questions:

1. Why is it important to preserve your family's heritage?

2. Why recipes?

3. What other traditions would you like to see preserved. Why?

4. What feelings do you have when you think of your favorite foods?

5. What things did you learn about your family in addition to the food traditions?

Keeping in Touch

Objective:

To remember a family member you don't often see.

Supplies Needed:

Stationery and pen/pencil or computer; art supplies such as paper, crayons or markers, etc.

Step-by-Step Instructions:

1. As a family, think of a relative you don't see very often.

2. Make a list of things you could tell her/him about or ask her/him in a letter.

3. Write the letter together. Some family members might like to design a card or make a picture to include.

4. Put everything together in an envelope or package and mail it.

5. E-mail is another way to keep in touch with distant relatives. All family members can be part of writing the e-mail message.

Discussion Questions:

1. Why is it important to keep in touch with relatives who don't live nearby?

2. How can the feeling of *family* be promoted or nurtured even when we are far away?

3. What other ways can we use to keep our extended family connected even though we don't see them often?

Sharing a 'Piece' of Me

Objective:

Work together to share a meaningful piece of each individual as a part of a total family project.

Supplies Needed:

Wall Hanging—A 6-inch or 9-inch square of plain fabric for each family member. Squares of colored fabric the same size as the plain fabric for piecing together and backing. May include batting between fabric. Fabric crayons, pencils, thread for sewing pieces together, dowel or curtain rod to use to hang if using as a wall hanging.

Step-by-Step Instructions:

1. To make a pieced family wall hanging: Decide on the size of the finished project. Any size squares can be used but squares that are 6-9 inches allow room for designs. Cut a square of plain fabric for each family member. Muslin works well. Also, check the directions on the fabric crayons for recommended fiber content.

2. Have each member use a pencil to design their square. They should include things about themselves such as interests, hobbies, talents, etc. They can use patterns to draw around or freehand design, depending on skills.

3. Follow directions on the fabric crayons as to how to color the design and heat set it.

4. Piece the squares together with alternating colored fabric squares to make the size of wall hanging desired. Or, the squares may be sewn together and then colored fabric sewn around the edge. Sew on backing with right sides together, leaving an opening to turn; may also sew fabric loops on the top to run a rod through to hang. Turn, stitch opening to close.

5. Press and hang.

Optional Project—Pillow Top:

Supplies Needed:

One 16- or 18-inch square of plain fabric, colored fabric for back; pillow square or fiber-fill for making pillow; thread, fabric crayons, pencils. (If sewing is not an option, iron in place with fusible web to make a wall hanging.)

1. Cut one big square of plain fabric, 16- to 18-inches.

2. Have each family member provide a design.

3. Follow direction on fabric crayons.

4. With right sides together, sew colored fabric to square, leaving an opening for turning.

5. Turn right-side out and press. Stuff. Slip stitch shut.

    Project can be displayed in the home, or given as a family gift to a special extended family member or friend.

    If the family does not have access to a sewing machine, this might be an opportunity to have help from a family member or friend who does have a machine. This demonstrates commitment as well!

Discussion Questions:

1. How does each family member make the family unique?

2. How can sharing individual interests and talents bring a family closer together?

3. How would the finished project look if one family member did not complete her/his block?

4. How does our family connect with others in the community?

5. In what ways does each family member show commitment to each other?

Keep in Contact

Objective:

To keep in contact with family members and talk about events, problems and activities.

Supplies Needed:

Cell phone or telephone calling card/computer messaging service.

Step-by-Step Instructions:

Choose a family time when family members can contact each other.

Discussion Questions:

1. When is the most convenient time for our family to make connections?

2. What are other ways to keep in touch?

3. What is "Plan B" if you cannot connect at the agreed upon time?

4. What does it mean to you and other family members to keep in touch on a regular basis?

5. How do you end your calls? Do you remind family members you love them?

The Family Tree

Objective:

To help children understand the connection they have with their family of past generations.

Supplies Needed:

Large sheet of paper (freezer paper or newsprint works well), pencils or pens, markers or crayons.

Step-by-Step Instructions:

1. Draw a large tree.

2. On the trunk of the tree, write your name.

3. On two of the branches above your name, write your parents' names, one on each branch.

4. Above them on two other branches, add your grandparents' names, your mother's parents above her name, and your father's parents above his name.

5. Keep going as far back as you can go.

6. Once you have all the names written on your tree, use markers or crayons to color your tree.

Discussion Questions:

1. How many of the people listed on the tree do you remember?

2. What do you remember about each person?

3. Ask grandparents, aunts and uncles what they remember about people listed on the tree.

4. See if you can locate pictures of the people on the tree. Copies of these pictures could be added as part of the design.

Source: *Building Strong Families: Choices and Challenges.* Columbia, MO: (1997). University of Missouri Outreach and Extension.

Family Time Capsule

Objective:

To help recognize that each individual has qualities and interests that can be combined to strengthen the family as it grows and continues through the life cycle.

Supplies Needed:

A durable container, paper, pencils and pens, small individual items representing the family and the individual members.

Step-by-Step Instructions:

1. This project is to put together a time capsule that the family will open and share at a designated time in the future. The family must work together to design the structure and identify desired contents of the capsule.

2. Each member may write a story, poem or goals for the future. Each individual may also want to select a special item and picture to include.

3. Another idea: Make a list of questions that each family member answers regarding interests, hobbies, favorite things and goals for the future.

4. The family may or may not want to share exactly what they have included, letting that be a surprise for the future.

5. It is important that each member feel a commitment to completing the capsule and sharing about herself/himself. Be sure to include all family members whether they live close or far away.

6. The family should decide how and where the capsule will be stored and when it will be opened. Possible times might be a high school or college graduation, wedding or wedding anniversary.

Discussion Questions:

1. Why is each family member's contribution important?

2. Is family commitment necessary to completing the capsule in a timely manner?

3. How might this capsule provide a positive way for the family to commit time together in the future?

Positive Communication

Before reading the next section, think about how your family communicates with each other; and, how you communicate as a couple. Fill out the communication inventory on the next page. You can then discuss your responses to the items, and talk about the strengths you demonstrate with each other and the areas of potential growth you would like to enhance. A planning guide is included so you can develop some goals. You might think about which of the activities at the end of this unit you want to complete for increasing the level of communication within your family and with your mate. You might even think about involving grandparents, significant others or other people important in your life.

American Family Strengths Inventory©

Positive Communication

Family members can record their perceptions here in the area of *Positive Communication*. Feel free to make copies of this page for each member of your family, or there are additional copies of this Inventory in the Appendix. Once each member has completed the Inventory, record their responses on the Tally Sheet provided in the Appendix.

You may want to complete this survey now, then again in three months and again in another six months. That way, you can see how your family is progressing.

Put an "S" for Strength beside the qualities you feel your family has achieved and a "G" beside those qualities that are an area of potential Growth. If the particular characteristic does not apply to your family or is not a characteristic that is important to you, put an "NA" for Not Applicable.

After recording your perceptions, spend some enjoyable time talking together about how your views are similar and how they are different. Remember: No one is absolutely right and no one is absolutely wrong on this. Everyone has a valid perception of what is happening and their views need to be considered carefully and respectfully. If you see ways to work together to enhance your strengths in the area of *Positive Communication*, feel free to jump in and do so in the coming days and weeks.

Family Member's Name:_____ Date:_____

In Our Family …

We feel comfortable sharing our feelings with each other.   _____

It is easy to understand each other's feelings.   _____

We like to talk openly with each other.   _____

We like to listen to each other.   _____

We respect each other's point of view.   _____

Talking through issues is important to us.   _____

We give each other a chance to explain ourselves.   _____

We enjoy our family discussions.   _____

We share funny stories together.   _____

Putdowns are rare.   _____

Sarcasm is not generally used.   _____

*All things considered, communication in our family is positive and
effective.*   _____

© Copyrighted material. For nonprofit educational purposes only. Not for resale.

Our Plan for Positive Communication

Now that you know your family's strengths related to positive communication, read the next section. As you read, you may want to think about how the examples fit your family. You can then look at ways your family might strengthen their communication with each other and write them in the space below. The activities at the end of this section are there to help you get started.

Our Plan

Based on our discussion about Positive Communication *in our family, we have decided to do the following things in the coming weeks and months to improve the way we talk to each other and listen to each other.*

1. _____

_____

_____

_____

2. _____

_____

_____

_____

3. _____

_____

_____

_____

Signed: _____   _____

       _____   _____

       _____   _____

Smoothing Out the Bumps in Family Life

Communication is on everyone's list of the qualities of strong families—open, honest, straightforward and clear communication. But **positive** communication—above all else—is the key to success.

One family therapist had to chuckle about a family she had worked with: "When I asked them if they felt their communication with each other was open, honest and straightforward and clear, they all agreed it was. The problem was, yelling at each other all the time may have all of the above qualities, but it still doesn't work," she laughed.

Dr. Nick Stinnett at the University of Alabama at Tuscaloosa likes to say: "In the world of words there is a way to say precisely what we would like to say, but in a positive manner that ensures that we will make progress in our relationship with each other." In short, stop and think for a few seconds how to restate your feelings in a way that is not hurtful to the other family member and will help to build your love for each other, rather than tear it down.

Of course, the most important talk in families often tends to be spontaneous talk. This is communication when no one is really working at communication, but simply enjoying talking and listening for talking and listening's sake. How does this young person in your family feel about sex? Or grades? Or her future? If parents and children are comfortable around each other and genuinely enjoy each other's company, then all kinds of interesting and important issues will come up in the conversation.

Communication in strong families does not always produce agreement on important issues. Family members are all individuals and have unique ways of looking at the world. It works best if they all can speak directly with each other without blaming or condemning. And even in strong families, some disagreements simply don't get resolved. People can still love each other and remain friends and loyal family members while agreeing to disagree on various issues. Religion and politics are two perennially hot topics, and the strongest of families can have members diametrically opposed in their world views. Do you want to see this type of situation as a terrible battle that just has to be fought and won, or as an opportunity for personal growth and interesting discussions? Take your pick.

There are ways to help increase the amount of positive communication within your family. Sometimes, it takes actually thinking about what you are saying and writing it down. One technique is to draw a line down the middle of a piece of paper. On one side, write all of the positive comments you make to family members. On the other side, write all the negative comments. The goal is to have at least 10 positive comments for each negative. Sound impossible? Here is the story of one father's attempt after attending a parenting class:

> I was determined to give all positive comments for a week to my 15-year-old son. Boy, was it tough to keep away from harping. I got through day one and by the second day, my kid was wondering what was wrong with me, all of that praise and no complaining. Thank goodness, it got easier for me as time went on. Then, on the fourth day, an amazing thing happened. My son and I were eating supper. Instead of leaving, like he usually does, he sat and we talked for another hour. We talked about things we hadn't shared for years. I hadn't been able to talk to my son like this in two years. My attitude and actions toward him really made a difference. I had no idea this would work.

Troubled families tend to be overly critical and hostile in their communication with each other, or deny problems and avoid verbal conflict. Either extreme gets families into trouble. A middle-ground approach, in which family members speak openly about their differences but have the grace to agree to disagree in some areas, generally works better.

Parents, of course, are in charge of the family. In some cases they will find it necessary to pull rank on the children or young adults in the family, making the final decision on important issues and sometimes overruling the younger family members. But this has to be done with skill and care, because no one—no matter how young or inexperienced they may be—likes to feel that their thoughts and feelings do not count for something.

Perhaps the best way to prevent communication difficulties in a family is for everyone to learn to be extremely good listeners. Communication, first and foremost, is about listening. As one father is fond of saying, "God gave us two ears and one mouth so we would listen twice as much as we talk. I sometimes think God should have given us 10 ears for every mouth. We would get along better as human beings." Family members in strong families are adept at asking questions and do not try to read each other's minds. They also know that people's views change over time, and the only way to avoid mind-reading is to check out positions regularly by asking questions.

In sum, positive communication in strong families is about sharing feelings, giving compliments, not blaming each other, being able to compromise and agreeing to disagree. We always need to remember that it's not about winning or losing arguments. It's about working together in the family so we all can feel loving toward each other and want the best for everyone.

Wants Are Never-ending

Dr. Karen Craig, a family economist, is fond of saying, "Wants are insatiable. The more you make, the more creative you are in spending." There never seems to be enough money; whether one makes a little bit of money or a lot, we can always find ways to spend more.

This creative genius never disappears, even in those times when family income is shrinking rather than expanding. But in tough times, it is especially important that family members remember to communicate with each other in positive rather than negative ways.

This is not easy to do, of course. Parents flush with money still find it difficult to keep their cool when faced with what may seem like a teenager's never-ending demand for the latest clothing or shoes so that the youngster can "fit in" with everyone else at school. In the best of times, $75 or $100 or $125 basketball shoes may seem excessive to a parent. In a year when net family business income is hovering at or near nothing, a request for such luxury items can easily drive a parent to the edge of distraction.

It takes a lot of practice for parents to figure out how to talk positively in situations such as these, but for the long-term well-being of the family, these challenging conversations need to be treated as opportunities for the parent to educate the young adult on money management, rather than simply blowing up and pointing out the child's ignorance.

Kids, in short, really have no idea what it costs to live, or how hard it is to make a living. And, it's very, very unlikely that they will really learn this, deep down and in great detail, until they go out on their own. But, parents can help their children begin the process by talking calmly with them about money. We could handle this type of situation by simply and firmly saying "No!" But the youngster isn't learning much from this, except that Mom or Dad is pretty crabby today. A better way would be to recognize that "fitting in" at school is important; that even though you are an "old person," by definition a parent, you still remember how important it is to be accepted by one's peers. The challenge for parents and children, together, is to figure out how the youngsters can fit in with their friends without doing further damage to a budget stretched way past its limit. So, who said parenting was easy, anyway?

For that matter, who said marriage was easy? One random sample of 2,555 American adults found that money was the most common issue people argued about in their families. Thirty-seven percent of the respondents said money was the major problem, followed by children and childrearing issues (29%), house-

hold chores (26%), and diets and health (21%) (Goodman, 1986). Family therapists point out, however, that arguments over money are often not really about
money at all. They are often actually battles over power and control in the family,
over competing hopes and dreams, over different visions of the good life and how
to live it.

Spouses argue about how money is to be spent or saved, and the disputes can
become pretty heated because they strike at core questions we pose to ourselves in
life:

- Am I earning enough to support my loved ones?

- If *he/she* makes the money (or most of the money) do I have any right to say
  how it should be spent?

- Who should help make financial decisions? The whole family? The partners?
  The wage earner?

- How important is money, anyway?

These questions, and countless other life situations in the household, need to
be discussed openly among family members. There are no easy answers, and
though it's easy to get upset with each other, the wisest course is to steer a positive
course through the minefields money can create in our materialistic society.

In the long run, the rewards of the human spirit—a sense of belonging and
connection with each other—tend to bring more happiness and satisfaction than
a life full of things. Psychologist David Lykken has studied happiness and
observes that, "People who go to work in their overalls and on the bus are just as
happy, on the average, as those in suits who drive to work in their own Mer-
cedes." Money is not important enough to fight about. But it is important
enough to talk about.

Listening and Speaking From the Heart

"Allen's been retired six months, and he's miserable. He was used to managing
several hundred people in his business, and now he sits at home and frets and
grumbles all day. He says he doesn't have any purpose in life. He drinks too
much. I worry he might harm himself."

For 45 minutes the woman discussed her husband's distress and her own feelings of inadequacy as she struggled in vain to find ways to help him. The counselor listened closely and suggested she contact a good counselor in her

hometown—one familiar with alcohol use—to work with both of them. The counselor added that she would likely find Al-Anon useful, and Alcoholics Anonymous might be helpful to him.

The conversation wouldn't have been particularly remarkable, except that she and the counselor had just met for the first time on a brief airplane flight. He sat down next to her, said, "How's life?" and she told him, in great detail.

What made this conversation remarkable was that they were total strangers, and, feeling that she was in a most difficult time in life, she found comfort confiding in another human being who expressed interest. Also, it was clear throughout the conversation that she hadn't talked with anyone else about her husband's situation. She carried the burden alone.

Good listeners often find themselves in conversations like that. "Bus stop intimacy": The desperate human need to connect with others, but done with strangers who will soon be gone.

Some might ask why this happens. Actually, there are a number of reasons. The art of self-disclosure is a fragile art and needs constant nurture to survive. As young children we learn quickly in the rough-and-tumble world that revealing one's genuine feelings about life can be dangerous. There are those who are quite willing to attack you, mistaking the human need for self-expression and connection as weakness. So, we learn to hide our feelings. We become chameleons, projecting whatever image we think the world wants to see of us, as if all is well. But the loneliness and feelings of disconnection can drag on us.

In a marriage we often get so caught up in survival issues—jobs, children, in-laws, broken-down cars and so forth—that time to sustain relationships is put on the back burner. We simply don't invest enough time in intimate communication with each other.

Power can also come into play in many marriages. The woman on the plane seemed to approach life with her husband like an employee rather than a spouse. He was used to being the boss at work, and he brought this attitude home to his family. Rather than enjoying his time with loved ones, he simply "managed" them. She had to walk softly and waste a huge amount of emotional energy puzzling over how to approach him on countless delicate issues. She often was caught between the adult children and her husband as the children struggled to control their own lives, and the husband tried to assert his authority over them.

The problem with applying a business management model in families is that few employees in the world love their boss, and few bosses love their employees. As employees, we may respect our boss (which sometimes simply translates to fear of the boss), but we aren't likely to genuinely love or even like the boss.

Love and friendship—what most of us are seeking in marital and family relationships—occur between equals. Love and friendship occur among family members when they invest time talking with each other, and when they make each other feel safe and valued as they express feelings.

Two important principles for nurturing positive communication in a family are: "Listen with your heart, and speak from the heart." Positive communication in families is open, honest, straightforward and kind. Family members listen respectfully to each other. The goal as a listener is not to gather information on others so that one can pounce upon them and win an argument and assert control. The goal is to better understand how the speaker sees the world and find ways to help the individual live a more fulfilling life. All this builds a warm, emotional bond among people.

Strengths-based Activities for Enhancing Positive Communication in the Family

Deep Questions

Objective:

To practice family conversation; to learn more about each other; to practice listening skills.

Supplies Needed:

None.

Step-by-Step Instructions:

1. Choose a time when the family is together and has time to relax. Mealtime may be appropriate, or an evening when family members don't have scheduled activities. (You may need to plan ahead and schedule a time.)

2. Take turns asking questions that will make family members stop and think. Listen carefully.

3. Let people follow up with another question, if appropriate.

4. Take turns answering each question. It will be fun to see the differences and the answers that are similar.

Possible Questions:

1. What was your favorite family trip and why?

2. What was the best thing that happened to you today?

3. What was the worst thing that happened to you today?

4. If you were given $500 to do anything you want, what would you do?

5. If we had a fire in our home, what would you do?

6. If you could meet any living person, who would it be and why?

7. If you could meet someone from history, who would it be and why?

8. Who is your favorite hero and why?

9. What is your all-time favorite movie (or television show) and why?

10. What do you value most about yourself? What would you like to improve?

11. What was your proudest moment?

12. What was your most embarrassing moment?

13. If you could have a whole day off from work or school and could do anything you wanted, what would you choose to do?

14. What community service project could your family do within the next month/year?

15. What do you like best about school or your job and why?

Discussion Questions:

1. How does it feel to take time as a family to just sit and talk?

2. What is one new thing you learned about someone in your family?

3. How does taking time to learn about each other help to strengthen your family?

4. How did you encourage each member to answer each question?

Developing Self-esteem

Objective:

To help parents and adolescent children to be able to see how much they know about one another and, it is hoped, learn some new things on the way. What's more, it can be fun!

Supplies Needed:

Pen/pencil and copies of the parent and child question pages.

Step-by-Step Instructions:

1. Select or rewrite the questions on pages 23-25 so they are appropriate for your family.

2. Copy both sets of questions for each family member.

3. Parents should answer the set of questions about their sons or daughters; children answer questions about their parent(s). Answer questions with what information you know.

4. At the same time, parents and children need to provide answers for their own sheet of questions. When everyone is finished, exchange and correct one another's worksheets.

5. Discuss each other's answers. You don't have to do all the questions at one time. The older the child, the more questions you can ask at one time.

Discussion Questions:

1. How well did you do?

2. Were these questions hard/easy to answer?

3. What did you learn that you did not previously know?

4. What surprised you about the right answers?

5. What feelings do you have now that you know the answers?

6. What more would you like to know about your parents/children? (Write down questions to ask another time.)

Family Cookbook

Objective:

Both immediate and extended family will enjoy and appreciate the communication that takes place during the sharing of family recipes. Family food traditions can be passed down through the sharing of family recipes. A useful family keepsake will result from this activity.

Supplies Needed:

Envelopes, stamps, letter to extended family members, recipe cards, stationery-type note cards, photograph album or scrapbook, camera, film, baking supplies and ingredients.

Recommended Time for Activity:

Over about a six-month time frame or flexible.

Step-by-Step Instructions:

1. Write to members of your extended family, asking them to participate in a Family Cookbook. To each family member, such as grandparents, aunts, uncles, cousins, brothers and sisters, send one or more recipe cards and stationery-type note cards.

2. Ask them to write their favorite recipes on the recipe cards. Explain that these should not be fancy recipes, but everyday recipes their family enjoys, longtime favorites, recipes passed down in the family. Also have them write a message on the note cards, including their signature, and a brief message about the recipe. Younger children can draw a picture of the family and their favorite food.

3. As the recipes come in, enjoy making each recipe with members of your immediate family.

4. Take a picture of the food before you eat it. Put the picture of the food, the note card and the recipe in the photograph album. Include pictures of family members, if possible.

5. Decide how you are going to distribute the book. Look at the strengths of your family members. Could someone design the cookbook and input all the information on the computer? Don't forget young family members who may have computer skills. You might have a family contest to create a book-cover design.

6. Check with local copy stores or printers to see how you can reproduce the cookbook for the best price. It may be cost-effective to print it from your computer and put it in a notebook.

7. Family members may pre-order books so you will know how many copies to make. Share the family cookbook at family reunions or holiday celebrations. You may want to find a place to have your completed book copied and put in a notebook. Take orders for a copy of this family cookbook.

Discussion Questions:

1. What foods do you remember eating when visiting relatives?

2. How many recipes came from different family members? Who submitted recipes? What special recipes are missing? Who would have them?

3. Are there any recipes that came from more than one person?

4. How can you pass recipes down from one generation to the next?

5. What was your favorite from among the foods prepared?

6. What recipes are based on traditional foods of your family's nationality?

7. Which foods would you make again?

8. How can you find the old favorite family recipes?

Family Greeting Cards

Objective:

To communicate with other family members near and far.

Supplies Needed:

Paper, markers, assorted craft materials as desired or computer card program.

Step-by-Step Instructions:

1. Design your own family or individual greeting cards. Make them for holidays, birthdays, thank-you or get-well occasions.

2. Create an address book that includes mailing addresses as well as e-mail addresses. Be sure to include all family members' addresses.

3. Make new cards when you run out!

Discussion Questions:

1. Why is it important to communicate with other people?

2. How do you feel when you get cards?

3. How do you think others will feel when they get a card from you?

4. When should you remember people with cards? Make a list of all events during a year. Beside each event, list the people you want to receive a card. Make notes on your calendar to remind yourself to send the cards.

Couple Investigation

Objective:

To get to know each other better.

Supplies Needed:

Pencil and paper.

Step-by-Step Instructions:

1. Make up a list of questions to ask your spouse. Here are some ideas:

   - If you could go anywhere in the world, where would you go and why?

   - If you could change one thing from your past, what would it be and how would that make your life different now?

   - Are you working in your dream occupation? If not, what would it be? How can you make your dream occupation happen?

   - What was the best/worst thing that happened to you as a child?

   - What did you do for fun when you were growing up? When did you do it last?

2. Guess what your spouse's answers will be before hearing her/his answers and write them down.

3. Compare your guesses with her/his answers to find out how much you really know about each other.

4. Ask positive questions about the answers. After learning answers to general questions about your partner, ask more questions about values. Just remember that we all don't share the same values and that is OK.

5. Save these questions and answers for five or 10 years and compare your responses from then and now.

Variations:

Use this activity during a long car trip so you have each other's undivided attention. You may want to use questions about the future. Where do you want to be working in five or 10 years? What will our couple relationship look like in five or 10 years? What changes do we want to make as a couple?

Discussion Questions:

1. How well did you guess the answers ahead of time?

2. What did you learn about your spouse that surprised you?

3. What insights did you gain from doing this activity?

4. Were there future plans (employment) you agreed on? Disagreed?

5. As a result of this activity, what changes do you want to make in your lives?

Family Post Office

Objective:

To encourage positive communication among family members.

Supplies Needed:

Manila envelopes or small boxes, markers, note paper and pens, sticky notes.

Step-by-Step Instructions:

1. Provide an envelope or box for each member.

2. Using markers or other media, each person should decorate an envelope or box to use as their mailbox. They should include their name as well any other designs that tell about interests or hobbies.

3. Select an area in the house where the envelopes can be hung or boxes placed so that they are easily accessed by everyone.

4. Throughout the week, each family member should write a note, poem or other message for each family member and put it in the envelope or box. The important thing is that it needs to be a positive message. Some weeks it may be easier to find positive things than others. A simple "I love you" or "Thanks for the great cookies you made this week" would work.

5. The family can decide if they want to share messages and how they share them. Also, they can decide if they want to sign their messages or not.

Discussion Questions:

1. How does looking for positive messages to share help improve attitudes?

2. How does receiving a positive message make you feel?

3. How does giving a positive message make you feel?

4. How do family members feel when they realize others really do recognize good things about each other or write a special poem that relates to another member?

5. Is it sometimes easier to put things on paper rather than say them directly to others? Why or why not?

6. Why is positive communication so important for families?

Variation:

Supply a pad of sticky notes for each family member. Encourage leaving special messages at different times and in different places. Example: Put one on the door just before someone leaves to go to work or school. Create a message scavenger hunt with special messages. This works great for children who are home alone after school. Encourage younger children to draw pictures if they cannot write.

Record-a-Letter

Objective:

To help young children to keep in touch with distant relatives.

Supplies Needed:

Tape recorder.

Step-by-Step Instructions:

1. Sit down with a tape recorder and have your child do one of the following:

    Read a favorite story. Pre-readers can do a decent—and very entertaining—imitation of reading.

    Describe her or his room. Spend extra time on favorite projects, new pictures or gifts from the relative you are recording for.

    Talk about an upcoming holiday. If it is to include a family gathering with the relatives, better yet!

    Sing a favorite song. You or your child can provide percussion effects in the background with a wooden spoon and an oatmeal container.

2. Your child can help package and mail the cassette.

Discussion Questions:

1. What are some other ideas for topics for a recorded letter?

2. What are other special things you can do to keep in touch?

Variation:

Write a letter or send an e-mail to relatives who live far away.

Make the Most of Family Meals

Objective:

To help parents gain strategies for enhancing communication at family meals.

Supplies Needed:

None.

Step-by-Step Instructions:

1. As a family, read the following tips on making the most of family meals together. Just sitting together at the table doesn't always lead to fascinating family conversations or warm mealtime memories.

2. Here are some ideas for building family traditions, improving communications and spending quality time together.

    It's Not *What* But *How* You Feed Your Family.
    Simple foods served with love and laughter will outshine gourmet goodies almost any time. A university food service manager tells of asking students for favorite family recipes. One student bragged about her mother's gravy. Though just a standard smooth gravy recipe, the manager proceeded to make it. The student said it wasn't as good as her Mom's. When Mom made it, it had all those delicious little lumps in it.

    It Doesn't Have to Be Fancy to Be Healthy!
    Healthy food doesn't need to be expensive or difficult to make. Tacos, a salad and frozen yogurt can be just as healthy for your family as a gourmet dinner.

    Start Slow, Learn as You Go.
    Don't try to go from no meals to nightly meals. Start with a couple meals together weekly. Find what works for your family and go from there.

    Take Turns Talking with a *Talking Stick*.
    If everyone in your family talks at once, take a tip from the Winnetka Alliance for Early Childhood. They suggest borrowing the *talking stick* idea from American Indians. They only allow the person holding the stick to talk. You might have a *talking cup* or other special item that gets passed from person to person, giving each the opportunity to speak.

    Don't Answer the Phone During Mealtime.
    How often are your meals interrupted by the phone? If you can't stand to ignore a ringing phone, either unplug it or turn off the ringer. Use an answering machine or voice mail if it's hard to refrain from responding to a

call. If there are some calls you need to answer immediately, such as those from an ill parent, get caller ID.

Turn Off the TV.

Encourage family members to star in their own lives and relate to each other rather than to some image on the TV screen. If there is an absolutely must-see show that occurs during dinnertime, tape it for later viewing.

Get Children Involved in Making Meals.

Children tend to have better appetites for food they help prepare. Plan, prepare and freeze meals ahead for busy evenings. Take advantage of family cooking times to really listen to your children.

Table Talk Tips.

Share positive things that have happened during the day. One family had a mealtime ritual in which everyone, including Mom and Dad, told one new thing they learned that day. Some families have a night where there's an assigned table topic. Here are some popular ideas:

- Describe something that happened recently that made you feel really happy.

- Someone gave you $1,000. You have to spend some of it on your family before you can buy anything for yourself. What would you buy for everyone?

- If you could live in a different time and place, where and when would you want to live? Why?

- If you could spend an afternoon with a famous person (living or dead) who would it be and why? What would you do?

Discussion Questions:

1. How many other opportunities besides family meals are available for you to communicate as a family? How important do you perceive family meals to be as an opportunity for communication?

2. What is one step and an implementation date you can commit to for enhancing family communications when eating together?

3. What is one time when your family really stood together with each other? How did you communicate?

4. How often does your family eat together now?

Final Thought:

If there's little time for you and your family to enjoy food and fellowship together, here's something to think about:

1. Imagine viewing a movie through your DVD on fast forward. You could see several movies in the time it takes to watch one at the normal speed. But, would you enjoy them as much? If your family's life is being lived in *fast forward*, maybe it's time to hit Stop or Pause—for several meals a week!

2. Identify some factors that interfere with family communication at mealtimes.

3. Discuss ways you can improve communication at family meals.

Money Clothesline

Objective:

The money clothesline is a way to show coin equations to young children so they can actually see, hear and *feel* what they are learning about money.

Supplies Needed:

Solid-colored fabric scraps (five different colors), a fabric marker, clothespins and a clothesline or heavy twine.

Step-by-Step Instructions:

1. Let the children help cut the fabric into squares:

    -   Color 1: ten 3-inch squares.
    -   Color 2: five 4-inch squares.
    -   Color 3: ten 5-inch squares.
    -   Color 4: four 6-inch squares.
    -   Color 5: one 7-inch square and one 2-inch square.

2. Use the fabric marker to draw as large a circle as possible on each square of fabric except for the 7-inch square and the 2-inch square.

3. Label the 3-inch circles to represent pennies, the 4-inch circles as nickels, the 5-inch circles as dimes, and the 6-inch circles as quarters.

4. On the 7-inch square, draw a rectangle and label it to represent a dollar bill. Draw an equal sign (=) on the 2-inch square.

5. String the clothesline between two chairs or across the corner of a room.

How to play with clothesline money equations:

1. Start with pennies. Ask your child to hang five "pennies" on the line.

2. Then show your child the equal sign and explain that it means "the same as." What are five pennies the same as? Five pennies are the same as one nickel.

3. Now the child hangs up the equal sign and one of the "nickels." Count the pennies again. Say together, "Five pennies are the same as one nickel."

4. As your child is ready, use the same steps to show coin equivalent statements for a dime and then a quarter.

For more challenge with the money clothesline:

• Write the money equations on slips of paper and put them in a basket. Let your child draw a slip of paper and see how fast the child can hang the equation on the money line.

• Have your child turn her/his back while you put on a *mystery* equation. Then let the child turn around and see how fast he/she can read the equation and lay out real coins to match.

• Add fabric squares to teach more skills.

Spending and Values

Objective:

To discuss how values differ in the family and understand how values influence spending; to serve as a further discussion on how money is spent in the family.

Supplies Needed:

Value sheet (included with the activity), pencils for each family member.

Step-by-Step Instructions:

1.   Have each family member complete the value sheet.

2.   Place the categories in order as an individual.

3.   Develop a *family total*.

Spending and Values

Everyone has values regarding money. But not everyone values the same things to the same extent. To help you recognize some of your own money values, read the pairs of words below. Circle one value in each pair that would be your first choice about how you would prefer to spend money. You must make one choice in each pair. Have each family member complete this activity. You will have a chance to compare your answers when you all have completed the activity. Make the assumption for this activity that you have enough to eat and a place to live.

If you had $50, what would you spend it on?

• Hobbies/Crafts/Tools	• Household Items	• Religion/Gifts
• Religion/Gifts	• Clothes/Personal Appearance	• Household Items
• Savings	• Savings	• Car/Gasoline
• Recreation/Social	• Religion/Gifts	• Food/Eating Out
• Food/Eating Out	• Clothes/Personal Appearance	• Food/Eating Out
• Religion/Gifts	• Religion/Gifts	• Hobbies/Crafts/Tools
• Hobbies/Crafts/Tools	• Religion/Gifts	• Household Items
• Clothes/Personal Appearance	• Recreation/Social	• Food/Eating Out

• Savings	• Car/Gasoline	• Clothes/Personal Appearance
• Hobbies/Crafts/Tools	• Savings	• Car/Gasoline
• Hobbies/Crafts/Tools	• Car/Gasoline	• Car/Gasoline
• Recreation/Social	• Household Items	• Recreation/Vacation
• Hobbies/Crafts/Tools	• Household Items	• Household Items
• Household Items	• Savings	• Recreation/Social
• Recreation/Social	• Food/Eating Out	• Religion/Gifts
• Household Items	• Recreation/Social	• Car/Gasoline
• Clothes/Personal Appearance	• Hobbies/Crafts/Tools	• Clothes/Personal Appearance
• Food/Eating Out	• Car/Gasoline	• Savings
• Food/Eating Out		
• Savings		

Count the times you circled Household Items and write the total in the space provided. Tally each of the other values the same way.

1. Household Items _____   5. Car/Gasoline _____

2. Food/Eating Out _____   6. Religion/Gifts _____

3. Clothes/Personal Appearance _____   7. Hobbies/Crafts/Tools _____

4. Recreation/Social _____   8. Savings _____

Write the item having the highest number in the space next to No. 1. If there is a tie, write the items in the order you would choose. The list reflects the items you consider most important in their order of importance. By knowing your values, you can design a personal spending plan that will fit them. The closer your spending plan fits your values, the easier it will be to follow.

1. _____   5. _____

2. _____   6. _____

3. _____   7. _____

4. _____   8. _____

Now see how you rank the items as a family. Add the numbers for each category and write the category with the lowest total next to No. 1. How closely does it reflect the order of your personal list?

1. _____   5. _____

2. _____   6. _____

3. _____   7. _____

4. _____   8. _____

Discussion Questions:

1. Did anything that came up high on the list surprise you?

2. Is there anything on the list that you wish would be higher? (An example might be savings.)

3. Did the couple or family list change from what you had as a personal list?

4. Did anyone have a much different list than the rest of the family?

5. Is there a difference between the parents and the youth?

6. Generally the items on the list are flexible expenses. If you add housing, utility and phone costs to the list, would the priorities change?

7. Would it be different if you had $100 to spend? $500 to spend?

8. Are there other categories you would like to see included in the comparisons?

9. As you develop your family spending plan, are there other items that need to be included in the plan? How about items that you might not need to spend as much on?

10. The closer each family member's personal list is to the total list, the less compromise is necessary. Will your family need to compromise a lot?

11. What did you learn about others in your family?

Take A Stand

Objective:

To help family members visually communicate feelings about money.

Supplies Needed:

Content statements, *Strongly Agree* and *Strongly Disagree* signs.

Step-by-Step Instructions:

1. Post *Strongly Agree* and *Strongly Disagree* signs on opposite walls.

2. Stretch a piece of tape or string on the floor from one sign to the other.

3. Tell family members to place themselves on the line continuum according to how they feel about the statements you will read. Tell them you will ask them to share why they stand where they do. Make a rule that the exact middle is not allowed for this activity.

Content Statements To Read (for ages 12 and up):

Colorado is the best place for our family vacation.

Florida is the best place for our family vacation.

California is the best place for our family vacation.

Smoking is not harmful to those breathing the secondhand smoke.

It is OK to drink as much alcohol as you want as long as you don't drive afterwards.

Credit cards are good.

People get in trouble when they borrow money.

Using credit costs less than using checks.

When we go on vacation, we need to have a credit card.

Playing card games is the best family activity we do.

Going for a walk is the best family activity we do together.

Caring for a pet is a good way to demonstrate you are responsible.

Washing the clothes is Mom's job.

Taking out the garbage is Dad's job.

Making the beds is (insert someone's name) job.

Raking leaves, shoveling show, etc., is Mom's job.

Making sure the car is filled with gas is Mom's job.

Planning meals is (insert someone's name) job.

Having a legal drinking age of 21 is a good thing.

Children should be required to work for the things that they want (with the exception of food and shelter).

Variation:

Try switching the content statements to another subject, such as sports, use of time or any topic of interest to your family.

Discussion Questions:

1. Ask family members to share their opinions after each statement is read and they have moved to their spot. Assure each one that it is OK to have different opinions. This is one way to illustrate how complex issues can be. If this activity is repeated at a later time, family members will find that opinions can change with changes in circumstances.

2. How did you feel about physically moving yourself to express your opinion?

3. What surprised you about this activity?

4. What can you learn from understanding people's thoughts about the use of money?

4-H Cooperative Curriculum System. (2002). Personal Finance Helper's Guide, Financial Champions Series. National 4-H Web site: http://pa4h.cas.psu.edu/FinancialChampions/

A Look Into Silence

Objective:

To learn to appreciate the challenge of communication when words don't work.

Supplies Needed:

None.

Step-by-Step Instructions:

1. Set aside a given amount of time (start with 10 minutes) during which you must communicate without speaking or using written communication.

2. Try to communicate about something ordinary: asking about the other person's day, talking about the weather, preparing a meal. Any topic is fine as long as there is no talking.

3. This game is a great way to begin to understand what many hearing-impaired or non-English-speaking people face every day.

Discussion Questions:

1. What was the hardest thing about not being able to talk?

2. What other forms of communication helped get the point across?

3. What can you do to be more understanding of those who cannot communicate with words?

Successful Management of Stress and Crisis

Before reading the next section, take a few minutes to see how you think your family is doing on successfully managing stress and crisis. Fill out the inventory that follows. As a family, or as a couple, discuss your responses to the items, and talk about the strengths you demonstrate with each other and the areas of potential growth you would like to enhance. A planning guide is included so you can develop some goals. The activities in this unit can help you gain some skills in handling stress. Some are geared toward your family, others are specifically for couples. Select those that seem the best for you.

American Family Strengths Inventory©

Managing Stress and Crisis Effectively

Family members can record their perceptions here in the area of *Managing Stress and Crisis Effectively*. Feel free to make copies of this page for each member of your family, or there are additional copies of this Inventory in the Appendix. Once each member has completed the Inventory, record their responses on the Tally Sheet provided in the Appendix.

You may want to complete this survey now, then again in three months and again in another six months. That way, you can see how your family is progressing.

Put an "S" for Strength beside the qualities you feel your family has achieved and a "G" beside those qualities that are an area of potential Growth. If the particular characteristic does not apply to your family or is not a characteristic that is important to you, put an "NA" for Not Applicable. After recording your perceptions, spend some enjoyable time talking together about how your views are similar and how they are different.

Family Member's Name:_____ Date:_____

In Our Family ...

A crisis has helped us grow closer together. _____

It is easy to find solutions to our problems when we talk about them. _____

It's important to try to change the things that we agree need changing, rather than ignoring the situation. _____

We can work together to solve very difficult family problems. _____

A crisis helps make our relationship strong. _____

We try not to worry too much because things usually work out OK. _____

We are able to face daily issues confidently. _____

We like to support each other. _____

Our friends are there when we need them. _____

A crisis makes us stick closer together. _____

We always find something good comes from a crisis. _____

We find it easy to make changes in our plans to meet changing circumstances.   _____

We have the courage to try to do new things in life that will improve things for our family.   _____

We can accept things in life that we know cannot be changed and find peace.   _____

All things considered, we look at challenges as opportunities for growth.   _____

©Copyrighted material. For nonprofit educational purposes only. Not for resale.

Our Plan for Managing Stress and Crisis Effectively

Now that you know your family's strengths related to managing stress and crisis, read the next section. As you read, you may want to think about how the examples fit your family. You can then look at ways your family might strengthen its ability to manage stress and crisis and write them in the space below. The activities at the end of this section are there to help you get started.

Our Plan

Based on our discussion about Managing Stress and Crisis Effectively, *we have decided to do the following things in the coming weeks and months to enhance our connections with each other as we deal with life's challenges together.*

1. _____

_____

_____

_____

2. _____

_____

_____

_____

3. _____

_____

_____

_____

Signed: _____   _____

           _____   _____

           _____   _____

A Stress Check List

Research on strong families across the country and around the world reveals useful approaches for dealing in a positive manner with stress and crisis in one's life. What follows is a list of strategies that tends to help families deal with stressful situations. Check the approaches your family uses:

_____   **We look for something positive,** and focus on that positive element in a difficult situation.

_____   **We pull together rather than apart.** We don't see the problem as an individual's problem, but as a challenge for the whole family.

_____   **We get help outside the family when we need it.** Help from extended family members, supportive friends, neighbors, colleagues, members of our religious community, professionals in the community. "It takes a whole village to resolve a crisis."

_____   **We create open channels of communication.** Challenges are not met when communication shuts down.

_____   **We keep things in perspective.** "These things, too, shall pass."

_____   **We adopt new roles in a flexible manner.** Crises often demand that individuals learn new approaches to life and take on different responsibilities.

_____   **We focus on what is most important and minimize fragmentation.** Without focus on the essentials, the details can get us edgy, even hysteric.

_____   **We give up on worrying, or put our cares in a box.** Worrying usually causes people more misery than the actual event they are worrying about. Sometimes it's best to stuff the worry down or resolve to worry 10 minutes a day and then forget it. The mind simply has to rest.

_____   **We eat well, exercise, love each other and get adequate sleep.** Often human beings forget that they are biological beings, not unlike kindergartners. We all need a good lunch, and we need to play. We need to have our hair stroked, and we need a good nap.

_____   **We create a life full of meaning and purpose.** All people face severe crises in life. We will not be able to avoid these challenges. Rather, our aim can be to live a useful life of service to our community. This brings a richness and dignity to our lives, in spite of the troubles we endure.

_____   **We actively meet our challenges head on.** Disaster in life does not go away when we look in another direction. But, it is also helpful sometimes to withdraw for a time and replenish ourselves.

_____ **We go with the flow to some degree.** Sometimes we are relatively powerless in the face of crisis. At this point it can be useful to simply "Let go, let God."

_____ **We are prepared in advance for the challenges in life.** Healthy family relationships are like an ample bank balance: If we have kept our relational accounts in order, we will be able to weather life's most difficult storms. Together.

_____ **We know how to laugh and we know how to cry**, for both are essential if we are to maintain an emotional balance in life.

_____ **We do not blame others for our fate**, but work with others to build a more satisfying world for all.

_____ **We take life's challenges one day at a time.** In especially tight situations, we sometimes need to take things one hour at a time, or perhaps one minute at a time.

_____ **We realize that suffering can be a catalyst for positive growth.** Crisis, by definition, is a difficult time in our lives. But it also can be a turning point, planting the seeds for a satisfying and successful future. This is hard to internalize, but useful to remember.

_____ **We identify spiritually with the grand procession of life:** Through good times and bad times we as individuals come and go, but life from whence we all spring is eternal. There is something satisfying and soothing about this thought.

In the space below, please add other useful approaches for managing stress and crisis that you have found helpful in your family:

1. _____

2. _____

3. _____

4. _____

Reframing the Situation

Strong families know how to manage difficult times in life creatively. Many counselors believe that one of the most important things a family can do in a time of crisis is to *reframe* the situation, i.e., look at what is happening to the family from a different perspective. For example, if a mother is a member of a National Guard unit that is being deployed outside the United States in a time of national uncertainty, this is clearly a significant challenge for the father, children, grand-parents and other loved ones left behind. Countless questions come up: Will Mom be OK? Can everyone left behind adjust to life without her for a while? And so forth.

But in many critical times, families often have little choice in the situation. Each individual family member can spiral down into depression or anger over the difficulty they will be facing when Mom leaves. Or, the family can hold a series of group discussions and focus on how they can work together to meet the challenges they face. They can find answers about how to maintain communication with Mom, even though she will be physically absent. In this way they can ensure that she is still a strong psychological presence in the family. Dad can figure out ways to adjust and hone his skills as a parent to new levels of competence. The kids can brainstorm ways they can contribute to the family's well-being and fill in the gaps caused by Mom's physical absence. Grandparents, often eager to con-tribute to the family's welfare, can offer suggestions on how they might be of help.

If the family can see the situation as not only a serious difficulty, but also as an opportunity to strengthen their bonds with each other, the challenge can be met. The key is positive communication with each other: Anything mentionable is manageable. In essence, if we can find the courage to talk with each other about a problem, we can find ways to solve it.

Families sometimes fall into disarray during times of crisis; but those families that can recover from the initial shock and sense of despair and band together to find solutions to their difficulties commonly say they feel stronger and more appreciative of each other as family members. "I wouldn't ever want to go through something like this again," people are likely to say, "but I wouldn't take a million dollars for the love we now share with each other as a result of our abil-ity to support and care for each other till the crisis was over."

Human beings have been relying on their creative ability to reframe difficult life situations for a long, long time. The Chinese symbol, or pictograph, for the word crisis is a composite of two other pictographs: the symbol for *danger* and the symbol for *opportunity*. For thousands of years, the Chinese have known that a crisis can be a dangerous time but also a time to look for new opportunities. Life can be even better and more fulfilling if we can find ways to endure hardships together.

The Chinese Symbol for Crisis

Danger   Opportunity

What the Experts Have to Say

The notion that a difficult time in life can be a catalyst for growth and a better life in the future is hard to swallow, especially when we are in the thick of hard times. Our first impulse often is to give up, run away, pull the covers over our heads, get mad, blame somebody else, self-medicate or do any of a host of other self-defeating things besides deal with the issue directly, honestly, intelligently, and with the help and encouragement of our loved ones.

Sometimes it's so hard we have to take life a day at a time. Sometimes we have to take it 10 minutes at a time. If we can just manage to hold on and do so with the support of the important people in our lives, the benefits are considerable and the wisdom we gain priceless.

Here is a collection of quotes from a group of experts—a group of normal, everyday people who have endured terrible losses in their lives and gone on living. What did they learn and what can they teach us?

> Life has ups and downs. And even when you feel there is no way you'll ever be up again, it does happen. Eventually.

—

> There are people who care about others. I wouldn't have survived without the support group, without my husband, without my kids, without the in-laws.

—

> I learned you may be able to beat me to the ground, but I won't stay there. I will be back.

—

I am a strong person. I can be responsible. It is going to take an awful lot to break me down. I am basically a survivor.

—

There comes an acceptance and understanding when you realize the growth you have experienced as a human being.

—

There is an awful lot I will never understand. No amount of analyzing, reading, studying will give all the answers. And that is all right. Life is worth living anyway.
I have learned that God loves me.

—

I learned that life is precious.

—

I learned that life is very short, and that you better enjoy it to its fullest while you have it.

—

I don't know what the future will bring. Life is full of uncertainties. You just have to take it as it comes.

—

Hopefully, the future will bring more growth for myself, both mentally and spiritually, with more peace in my soul, more compassion and understanding for myself and other people.

Each human being experiences difficult times in life, and each of us deals with the situation in our own unique way. We rise above our difficulties by relying upon our social, emotional and spiritual resources. When studying stress and crisis for a long time, it is hard for a researcher not to conclude that human beings and human families can be remarkably resilient, and we do ourselves a considerable disservice by failing to recognize the power we have to transcend life's challenges. Our species would not have survived through the millennia if we were not quite gifted when confronted by difficulty.

By Helping Others We Help Ourselves

There are two great secrets in the 21st century: first, that we all suffer; and second, that suffering can be a catalyst for growth in our lives. Perhaps these secrets aren't really secrets at all. In fact, they are widely known, but we often forget them when times get tough.

Many people try to cope with life's difficulties by reaching for alcohol, other drugs and other ways to mask human pain. These sometimes bring short-term relief, but in the long-run they most often make things worse and bring us to the brink of disaster, and past. Alcohol and other drugs are a way we try to change channels in life, to turn on another station in our brains, to take away the misery we feel. Some people do this by purposely hurting themselves—physically injuring their bodies, savaging their souls. This doesn't work.

A better way that counselors often recommend is to focus on the needs of others. Rather than wallow in our own problems, dedicate our lives to helping make the world a better place and the lives of others more fulfilling. By doing so, we take our own minds off our problems, learn that countless humans on earth are troubled, and that by working together we can conquer just about any difficulty. Many people believe that God works through us in this way. Some who have difficulty with the word God, for a variety of reasons, think about connecting to an important cause in life that brings meaning and purpose, and this sense of connection gives us hope and peace.

Whatever terms we use, the psychological dynamic is similar: focusing on something important, something above the petty, mundane and cranky world we can often descend into.

Parents who have lost children will often say that they wanted to die, or they just wanted to go to sleep and make the pain go away, but they were saved by the surviving children in their family. Without the need to get out of bed each morning and take care of the other children, these parents are convinced they would have sunk into a hopeless despair that knows no depth. And, it's amazing how young we learn the importance of caring for each other. One Mom whose baby had died told how she cried and cried and cried, most often alone with the bedroom door closed. One morning her three-year-old daughter saw her tears and crawled up on her lap: "Don't cry, Momma," the child fretted. "I'll take care of you!" The mother gained comfort and strength from the little girl: "She helped pull me through the crisis."

A crisis in life is a time when we become lost and alone. We sink into the feeling that no one has suffered the way we are suffering, no one could possibly understand our despair, and there is no hope of this despair ever ending. The fact is, we all suffer. Our tragedies are unique and different in many ways, but deep down we share common feelings of loss and despair. It's not wise to tell someone that "I have gone through the same thing," or "I understand your feelings perfectly," because we don't. But, we understand enough about tragedy and tragic feelings in life to be drawn to each other, to want to help each other, to want to be with each other on the long journey to healing.

In the final analysis, living through despair teaches us all that there are good people in the world and we can reach out to them and receive support when we need it. And then, when our own crisis has for the most part subsided, there will be other people in the world whom we can care for in return for the kindness we received earlier. The law of distributive justice holds that in the end, we give what we get, we get what we give, the love you receive will be equal to the love you have freely given.

Strengthening Families and Communities in Times of Crisis and Uncertainty

Dr. David H. Olson notes that all of the problems in the world either begin in families or end up in families. The crises following the bombing of Pearl Harbor, 9/11, the southeastern tsunami, Hurricane Katrina and other world tragedies caused untold damage to family and community well-being. Feelings of despair abound in such situations, and yet the impulse to step forward and help in some way is strong.

Working Together Rather Than Pulling Apart

The immediate reaction in this country and many others during a time of crisis has been to look to each other for solace. Families come together to watch events develop on television. Our friends at work, many of whom are like family to us, share their grief and we feel closer to each other. The need to lean on each other is strong. Even in the greater community that we share with strangers, there seems to be a more pervasive spirit of common humanity. We seem more solicitous to each other at the supermarket, more willing to offer a kind word and a polite demeanor at the florist.

However, when the shock of tragedy begins to wear off, we are likely to return to our more cantankerous and very human behaviors. Our common grief becomes supplanted by hardened individualistic visions of military and political strategy and tactics. The tone of public discussion becomes shrill once again. We all are aware of the pattern: The delicate weave of common humanity in a despairing time is likely to return to the tribal warfare that abounds.

Strong families rise above crisis by working together toward a common goal. In times of crisis, we can be especially sensitive to each other's feelings and needs. In our communities we can strive to connect with each other rather than spending so much energy on winning some kind of self-imposed race we have decided to construct against our competitors. We can reach out rather than push away. All things considered, we are a family: a very human family.

Strengths-based Activities for Developing Coping Ability in the Family

Do a Don't Do List

Objective:

To help couples and family members find time for the activities that are most important to them.

Supplies Needed:

Paper and pencil for each person.

Step-by-Step Instructions:

1. Have each person do the following exercise:

    *   Draw a large circle on your piece of paper.

    *   Look at the circle you've drawn and think of it as a clock with 24 hours. Halfway around would equal 12 hours.

    *   Put a dot at the top of the circle and label that dot with the time you get up to begin your day.

    *   Put a second dot at the point on the circle proportional to the number of hours later when you go to bed.

    *   Draw a pie-shaped wedge to the center of your circle from the two dots. For example, if you sleep about eight hours, your "sleep section" will fill about one third of your 24-hour clock.

    *   Next, quickly think through a typical day. Divide the rest of the clock into wedges that show how much time is spent in other activities. Label the different areas: work, eating, studying, meal preparation, commuting, personal grooming, working around house, watching TV, exercising and so forth.

2. Discuss how you spend your days. Were there any surprises? For example, did you discover you spend very little time together as a couple or family?

3. Now that you've identified the blocks of activity that fill your days, discuss if this is the way you enjoy spending your time. What things would you like to do more of as a couple or family if you had more time?

4. Rather than develop a *To Do* list, write a *Don't Do* list. This might include watching television, taking part in activities without your family, buying more things so there are more items you have to clean, fix, service, etc.

Discussion Questions:

1. What is one activity you and your spouse/family can commit to right now that you would like to do more of together?

2. What activities would have to go on a *Don't Do* list to make this happen?

3. How are you going to implement your decisions?

4. When are you going to implement your plan?

Heads Together

Objective:

To provide a relaxed time to talk over difficult issues.

Supplies Needed:

None.

Step-by-Step Instructions:

1. When families are in the middle of a difficult situation, whether it's coming to agreement on limits for children or teens or talking about issues like drugs, alcohol, tobacco, etc., having some relaxed time to talk can make a big difference. Set aside at least one hour when no one has other activities planned.

2. Turn off the television, let the answering machine take telephone messages. Quiet background music may help, but don't let it be a distraction.

3. Often times, lying down and looking at the ceiling—or at the sky—can help open communication lines and add to the feeling of being relaxed and non-confrontational.

4. The idea is to just talk. Begin by stating the question, issue or problem clearly. Whether it's two family members or four or more, each person gets a chance to state their feelings, ideas, opinions or to ask questions. If the feeling becomes tense, remind each other to take a deep breath before you continue.

I messages can help in tense situations, too. Fill in the blanks below, focusing on how *I* feel and what *I* would like, not on *you*.

When this happens _____

I feel _____

Because _____

I would like _____

This may feel strange to begin with. Just take time. Try it. Don't feel like anything profound has to be said. Just speak from the heart—and listen with your heart.

Discussion Questions:

1. What did we learn from our time together?

2. What was the hardest thing about it?

3. What did you like best?

4. What other topics should we talk about in this way? (If you think of other things, you may want to set an appointment for the next *Heads Together* session.)

Juggling Choices

Objective:

To teach the importance of time management and the effects that over-involvement has on one's life.

Supplies Needed:

Two to four round balloons (about 9 inches in diameter) for each family member.

Step-By-Step Instructions:

1. Blow up two balloons for every family member.

2. Family members will need to get in a circle.

3. Start with one balloon. Have the rest of the balloons close at hand.

4. As a group, juggle the balloon. The idea is to keep the balloon from hitting the floor. As the group figures out how to keep the balloon under control, start adding balloons one or two at a time.

5. Start over as necessary when balloons hit the floor.

Discussion Questions:

1. How can we compare our own lives to the activity of keeping the balloons in the air?

2. How many balloons as a family can we successfully juggle?

3. Have everyone list their activities and responsibilities.

4. Are some activities and responsibilities more important than others to you? To others? Which ones?

5. What happens when we have too much going on?

6. How is that like juggling the balloons?

7. What are the strategies we used to keep the balloons in the air?

8. What are some of the strategies we use to keep up with our activities or responsibilities?

9. How do we know when we are *too busy*?

10. Have you become so busy that you do not have time to just *kick back*?

11. When this happens, what can you do to have a more relaxed life?

12. How can our family better juggle our activities and responsibilities?

Neighbors in Distress

Objective:

To practice thoughtfulness toward others who are going through difficult times.

Supplies Needed:

Depends on which activity your family chooses.

Step-by-Step Instructions:

1. Talk about ways to help others when they have a crisis in their life. This can be things you could do as a family or as individuals. Think about your extended family, your neighbors and your friends.

2. Think of someone you know who is having a hard time right now. Use one of your ideas for helping and try it out. (Bake and deliver a plate of fresh cookies, offer to babysit, send a card with a handwritten message, etc.)

Discussion Questions:

1. How did it feel to do something thoughtful for someone else? What was the best part about doing it?

2. Why is it so hard to offer help to others? How can we make it easier to do?

3. What can we do on a regular basis to help others?

Prepare for the Unexpected

Objective:

To learn skills to deal with emergencies and other unplanned situations; to take time to practice skills needed in case of emergency.

Supplies Needed:

Various supplies, depending on the skill to be learned.

Step-by-Step Instructions:

1. Make a list of skills that might be needed in case the unexpected happens. Some skills family members need to learn:

    *   Social skills: How to answer the phone and take messages, how to answer the door.

    *   Safety and survival skills: How to escape a home fire, how to give first aid, what to do if the power goes out, how to call 911.

    *   Car care: How to handle a breakdown on the road, how to change a tire, what to do in case of a car accident.

    *   Household care: How to do the laundry, how to keep the house clean, how to do easy home repairs.

    *   Preparing meals: How to make some simple meals, how to use the oven, microwave and other appliances.

    *   Managing money: How to balance a checkbook, how to pay bills, how to set up a budget, how to count change.

2. Decide which skills are most important and who in the family needs to learn them.

3. Make a plan for how to proceed.

Discussion Questions:

1. When might we need to know this skill?

2. How can being prepared help us all stay calm when something unexpected happens?

3. What if? (Practice various *what if?* scenarios to help family members think ahead about what needs to be done in a specific situation.)

Source: *Building Strong Families: Choices and Challenges.* (1997). Columbia, MO: University of Missouri Outreach and Extension

Supporting Each Other Through Daily Life

Objectives:

Family members will listen and care about each other's stressors or things that upset them. They will each do their part in helping each other cope with stress and make it through the difficult times that all family members face on occasion.

Supplies Needed:

Construction paper and crayons.

Step-by-Step Instructions:

1. Each family member should think of one thing that is stressful.

2. Children may have a difficult time talking about stress so you may need to help them think of one thing they do not like or that makes them feel bad or unhappy. Elementary children may want to draw pictures of things that cause stress.

    Some examples for children might include:

    *   Being late for school.
    *   Not being picked for a team.
    *   Not having any clean jeans.
    *   Not being able to find a tennis shoe.
    *   Losing a library book.
    *   Waking up tired in the morning and not wanting to get out of bed.
    *   A younger sibling has gotten into your stuff.

3. Ask, "What can you do to make the situation better?"

4. "Are you upset about things that you cannot change?"

5. "What can we do to help each other?"

6. Have the children draw pictures or talk about things they can do together to make life less stressful. For children, you may need to use simpler words like *happy* and *feel good*. Use your imagination when children express their stressors to you and brainstorm together how some problems may be relieved.

7. Parents can also participate by drawing a picture and talking about things they can do to make life less stressful for the family. Questions for parents to consider:

   • "What does the word *stress* mean?"

   • "Is some stress good or OK?"

   • "When is too much stress not healthy?"

   • "How can we help each other relieve some stress?"

8. No matter how you design the activity, the main goal is to increase communication among family members about stress, and to develop ways to help each other in difficult times.

Relaxing Together

Objectives:

Families will learn together how to better manage the stress in their lives, and will practice skills they can use both for family stress and for stress at school or work.

Supplies Needed:

Some quiet time; music (piano or other musical instrument, CDs or tapes and player).

Recommended Time for Activity:

Once a week for about a half hour or less, until skills are learned and can be applied by all family members when needed.

Step-by-Step Instructions:

1. For each session, family members gather in a *quiet place*. They may sit or lie on a bed or couch or the floor.

2. One family member can explain the activity for the week, and all can do the activities together. Get comfortable. Talk in low, calm voices.

    Week 1—Audio and visual focusing. Close your eyes, and keep them closed for five minutes (if children younger than age seven are in the family, five minutes will be too long, reduce this to three). Focus your thoughts on what you can hear. It may be the hum of the furnace, the wind, animals or other small sounds. Have each family member tell what they heard. Try again, this time with visual focusing. Look at something in the room, or better still, something at a distance outside. Focus on it and think about its shape, size, color, etc. Ask each family member to describe the object they focused on.

    Week 2—Tape Player in My Mind. Explain that we have thoughts running through our minds all the time, a little like a tape player. If we run positive thoughts, we manage our stress better. If we run negative thoughts, we have more difficulty with stress. Be quiet and think about the kinds of thoughts you have. Share this with the rest of the family. Talk together about ways to make the thoughts more positive. Negative thoughts are: "I can't do this," "It's too hard," "I'll never succeed." Positive thoughts are: "I'm getting better at this," and "I can manage this."

    Week 3—Vacation in My Mind. Each person closes their eyes. Think about a place that you particularly like or a place you'd like to go to that you've never visited. Think about the sights, sounds, smells of this place. Focus on what it would be like to be there. Each family member can explain where they went on their vacation in their mind. Emphasize that this is not the same as day-dreaming but is a way to focus thoughts.

    Week 4—Deep Muscle Relaxation. Everyone lies on the floor, on their back if possible. Hands loosely at sides, feet relaxed to the side, head to the side, eyes closed. One person with a soft, soothing tone gives these instructions: "Think about your toes. Wiggle them. Then, let them relax and go soft. Think about the muscles across the bottom of your foot. Let them relax. Move up to your ankles. Relax, relax, relax. The calf muscles may have a lot of tension. Relax them. Then your knees. Thigh muscles are large. It will take more to relax them. Give yourself some time. Your body should start to feel like a soft rag doll." Move on up the body with instructions similar to those given above. Do fingers, wrists, lower and upper arms, lower back, upper back, shoulders, neck, across top of head, sinus area, stomach, hips, back down to toes. This method of relaxation takes some practice to be able to let your muscles truly relax, but can be used for a lifetime of better sleeping and to put your body at ease whenever you are feeling stressed.

Week 5—Music Lovers Stress Reliever. Play your family's or your own favorite music for at least a half hour. Play some of each family member's favorite songs. Sing along, particularly as a group. You can also dance to the music.

Discussion Questions:

1. How does each activity help you manage stress better?

2. How can the family help each other to manage stress better?

3. Do you feel less stressed after listening to music?

4. When would be the best time to use each type of stress management technique?

Remember When

Objective:

Help children develop confidence and a sense of self-worth that carries them through trying times.

Supplies Needed:

Inexpensive photo album for each child with *magnetic* peel-back plastic pages; doubles of snapshots.

Step-by-Step Instructions:

1. As you take photos of your children, family, significant places or activities in their lives, remember to print doubles and pull out copies for a photo book.

2. Pick out the photos that will be the most memorable for each child. You only need one or two of an event. The idea is to trigger memories, not be all-inclusive on the details. Put the date on the back for future reference.

3. Put the photos in the book. Peel-back pages are quick and more durable than gluing or photo corners. Captions are not necessary. (Photos for all children

can be put in one book or they can each have their own, depending on your time and financial resources.)

4. The key is to store these books where children can take them out and look at them often. These are not books to be kept for adulthood. They are to be used like storybooks and looked at until they are worn out! Take time to sit with them at least some of the time when they look at their book and talk about the photos; they can also look at their book alone. (Even teens like to look back to the times when they were little and talk about specific events they remember. It can be reassuring at times when they struggle in other areas of their lives.)

Discussion Questions:

Ask questions that will help them remember that time of their life to reinforce how they have grown and matured as well as to help them realize what their support systems are. For example:

1. What do you remember best about that time?

2. Why did we do that (activity)?

3. What made that (event or activity) fun?

4. Who is in the picture? What do you remember most about what was happening then?

5. Who do you see that you can go to when you feel down?

6. How have you grown or changed since then?

The Family Quilt

Objective:

To create a sense of unity among separated family members.

Supplies Needed:

Scraps from old clothing from each family member.

Step-by-Step Instructions:

1. Creating a quilt from old clothing belonging to family members can be a healing process for families who like to quilt. (If there are questions about how to quilt, many books are available at the library.)

2. If a family is experiencing a divorce, cutting and sewing together quilt squares from clothing of all family members (both from families of origin and blended families) can represent the new relationships that are being formed.

3. If a teenager is leaving home, the quilt can represent the family support he/she has from home.

4. When a family is dividing up belongings after the death of parents, a quilt made from old clothing can preserve years of memories.

5. During the quilting process, many family stories will probably be told, and families may want to write down or tape these stories to go along with the quilt.

Variations:

Putting old and new pictures of family members on fabric is also possible. These could be sewn together to make a family quilt. Young children could make paper quilts by drawing pictures on construction paper squares and taping them together or gluing them to a piece of paper. Pieces of fabric may be cut from the clothing and added to the picture.

Discussion Questions:

1. How is this quilt like our family?

2. How can you use this quilt when you are feeling sad?

3. What memories do you have that are related to each family member represented in the quilt?

Making a Savings Bank

Objective:

To learn a way to teach children how to make saving money a habit and to teach them the importance of delayed gratification.

Supplies Needed:

Plastic soft drink or water bottle or other container that can be used to make a child's bank.

Step-by-Step Instructions:

1. Piggy banks made from clear, see-through materials are best for children because they can see their money grow. Look around the house for containers that you can use to decorate and personalize for each child's bank.

2. One idea is to use a plastic soft drink or water bottle. Cut a slit in the side.

3. Laying bottle horizontally, use items such as corks for the feet, a pipe cleaner for the tail, a cap for the nose, felt for the ears and markers to draw the face.

Discussion Questions:

1. When making the bank, talk about ways to spend the money.

2. How much allowance might be saved each week?

3. How long will it take to save for a particular item?

4. How can you earn money to increase the savings?

   Once you have completed the bank, place it in a prominent place and monitor and encourage your child to add to the bank on a specific day each week so saving becomes routine.

5. How often do you put money in the bank?

6. Why is it good to always have money saved?

7. Has there ever been a time where you needed money but didn't have it?

    When enough money has been saved to purchase the desired item, discuss whether or not the child still wants it.

8. Was it worth the wait?

9. How does the child feel now that he or she can actually have what he/she has been saving for?

10. Talk about other items/activities the child would like to save money for.

Spiritual Well-being

Before reading the next section, think about the spiritual aspects of life in your family. Take the following assessment to see how you are doing. You can then discuss your responses to the items, and talk about the strengths you demonstrate with each other and where you would like to improve. A planning guide is included so you can develop some goals. The activities at the end of this unit are designed to help family members enhance the family's spiritual well-being. Some are geared toward your family, others are specifically for couples. Select those that would work best for you.

American Family Strengths Inventory©

Spiritual Well-being

Family members can record their perceptions here in the area of *Spiritual Well-being*. Feel free to make copies of this page for each member of your family, or there are additional copies of this Inventory in the Appendix. Once each member has completed the Inventory, record their responses on the Tally Sheet provided in the Appendix.

You may want to complete this survey now, then again in three months and again in another six months. That way, you can see how your family is progressing.

Put an "S" for Strength beside the qualities you feel your family has achieved and a "G" beside those qualities that are an area of potential Growth. If the particular characteristic does not apply to your family or is not a characteristic that is important to you, put an "NA" for Not Applicable. After recording your perceptions, spend some enjoyable time talking together about how your views are similar and how they are different.

Family Member's Name:_____ Date:_____

In Our Family ...

We have a hopeful attitude toward life. _____

Our home feels like a sanctuary for all of us. _____

We have a strong sense of belonging. _____

We enjoy learning about our family history. _____

We feel strong connections with our ancestors _____

There is a feeling of safety and security. _____

We feel connected with nature and the world around us _____

We feel a strong connection with the land. _____

There is a sense of peace among us. _____

We believe that love is a powerful force that keeps us together. _____

We benefit in many ways from our belief in a higher being or power. _____

It is easy to share our spiritual values and beliefs with each other.   _____

Our personal religious beliefs are compatible with each other.   _____

All things considered, we have strong spiritual connections that enhance our well-being.   _____

©Copyrighted material. For nonprofit educational purposes only. Not for resale.

Our Plan for Spiritual Well-being

Now that you know your family's strengths related to spiritual well-being, read the next section. As you read, you may want to think about how the examples fit your family. You can then look at ways your family might strengthen their spiritual well-being and write them in the space below. The activities at the end of this section are there to help you get started.

Our Plan

Based on our discussion about spiritual well-being, *we have decided to do the following things in the coming weeks and months to enhance our connections with each other.*

1. _____

_____

_____

_____

2. _____

_____

_____

_____

3. _____

_____

_____

Signed: _____   _____

_____   _____

_____   _____

Sacred Connections

A few years ago, a family researcher was having tea with Bryson, an older gentleman, in the dining room of his modest home in New South Wales, Australia. Bryson's wife of many years, Joan, had died of cancer eight years before. "Do you still feel connected to Joan?" the researcher asked. "Oh, yes," Bryson replied. "She's right here in the room with us now."

This is often heard from people in strong families. "She's with me a lot," Bryson continued. "She comforts me and looks over me, and makes it possible for me to go on in life in this world without her. I would have ended it all a couple years ago if Joan wouldn't have been with me."

Bryson had a profound and deep emotional connection with his wife Joan, a connection similar to the one another woman, Louise, has for her mother. Louise's mom died when she was 15 years old, but a powerful bond still lives in her heart today. "Sometimes when I'm feeling sad, and sometimes when I'm feeling happy, I'll go out to the cemetery and talk with Mom," she says. "I tell her how life's going and tell her how much I miss her. I know it sounds crazy, and I don't tell many people about it, but it gives me great comfort."

Ordinary words don't do this bond justice, and in the model of family strengths, the phrase spiritual well-being is used to describe this sacred connection. Years ago researchers talked about religion as a family strength, but thinking evolved and the term spiritual well-being seems to work better.

People tend to associate the term religion with institutions and doctrine. For many people, these associations are quite positive. For others, the term conjures up negative images often going back to childhood. Besides, the term religion isn't really broad enough to describe what strong family members have been describing.

Some families talk about faith in God, faith in life, faith in loved ones. They talk about being generally hopeful about life and believe that, in a broad sense, life works out pretty well for them. Some describe a feeling of oneness with the world, a connection to nature, to the land. Some people talk about how important it is to them that family members share important ethical values and beliefs, and express themselves in these terms by commitment to important social causes.

And then there are the Brysons and Louises of the world who talk about their families in almost religious terms, describing the love they feel for one another as sacred and selfless. What profound force drives parents to dive into raging torrents to rescue a child in distress without the slightest consideration for their own personal safety?

Spiritual well-being comes from the caring center within each individual that promotes sharing, love and compassion. Spiritual well-being is the feeling or power that helps people transcend themselves, rising above the mundane and petty to identify with the greater good: "I feel my family is a part of all the families of the world," said one individual.

Membership in a religious institution or spiritual group can provide a caring, supportive community to help when illness strikes, a baby is born or an accident occurs. Friends in the group are often quick to help each other. But many strong families are not involved with such an institution. In some countries, a relatively small percentage of families go to a church or synagogue or mosque or temple on a regular basis, but many families still nurture a sense of spiritual well-being in their lives.

Talking About Religion and Spirituality in Families

When David and Marian welcome visitors into their home, it is readily apparent that religion is important in their lives. The first thing we see in the foyer is an ornate antique cherry wood table covered with an elaborately crocheted white cloth. A large family Bible, passed down through several generations, rests on the table, opened to a favored passage, 1st Corinthians 13:4: "… Love is patient and kind." The message intended upon seeing this altar and reading these words is quite clear: The family's home is a sacred place, and all who enter will be treated with kindness.

David is a kind, deeply religious man with a gentle sense of humor. At one point, David received a letter from his son James. James is 23 years old and away at graduate school. It was an eight-page letter telling in detail why he doesn't believe in God. This is not an atypical story. There are countless examples of religious disputes in families. Often, the son or daughter goes off to the university, begins to question the family's faith, and ends up in a fierce argument over Thanksgiving turkey when he or she comes home to visit.

In his letter to his father, James expressed his need to create a belief system that is meaningful to him personally. David's response comes from a perspective that isn't commonly heard.

Rather than writing back an angry letter that is argumentative, David comments:

> Take a look. See how well he writes, and his thinking is very logical. … You
> know, when I was young, I went on my own spiritual journey and found a

way that works for me. James is clearly on his own spiritual journey right now. He has expressed some very personal thoughts. He is finding his way in the world. I can share my own beliefs, which are very, very important to me, and different from his. But I can't make him believe something that makes no sense to him. The best thing I can do is love him and listen to what he's thinking. It would be terribly sad to me if he couldn't talk with his father about religion. It's such a vitally important topic.

By keeping the lines of communication open with his son, David has found a way to maintain family ties without stifling individual differences. Though difficult, David's approach can be effective. By stifling individual differences in families, the ties are not made stronger but start to unravel.

What often happens is that young people, fearing an angry or sorrowful response from their parents, simply close the parents off. When parents over-react to a young person's searching questions, the young person quickly learns not to bring up anything important: "It will just make Mom mad." The parent may feel that different beliefs are a sign of disrespect and betrayal. More likely, they are evidence of human intelligence at work: By searching and questioning, we create new ways of looking at the world, and sometimes the quality of life is dramatically improved by using our natural human curiosity to good advantage.

Strengths-based Activities for Developing Spiritual Well-being in the Family
Service Calendar

Objectives:

To discover the joy of serving others; and to work and spend time together as a couple or family to do something from which someone else reaps the benefit.

Supplies Needed:

Calendar, pencil.

Step-by-Step Instructions:

1. Regardless of religious affiliation, serving others is considered a virtue. Help family members understand the joy of serving by developing a service calendar for the year.

2. At the beginning of the year, brainstorm ways your family could serve others throughout the year.

3. Mark it on your calendar as a reminder. Ideas to get started: January—Donate outgrown coats and mittens to a homeless shelter. February—Valentine caroling at a nursing home. March—Offer to clean out winter debris from an elderly neighbor's flower beds.

Discussion Questions:

1. How does it feel to think about the needs of others?

2. How does your serving affect the recipients?

3. If someone were going to serve you, what would you appreciate the most?

4. How did our project go?

5. What was the best thing about it?

6. What should we do differently next time?

7. Why is it important for us to do projects like this?

8. How does doing community service demonstrate what is important to your family?

9. What other ideas do you have for things you could do in your community?

10. Should we ask others to help on our next project? If yes, who?

11. How did this project help you learn more about each other?

Helping Others

Objective:

To help your children learn compassion by choosing a family project to help others.

Supplies Needed:

Time and energy.

Recommended Time for Activity:

Will depend on the project chosen.

Step-by-Step Instructions:

1. Some communities have *Sharing and Caring* days that identify a need in the community and a program to meet the need. As a family, discuss organizations in the community that help others.

2. Choose an organization and call to see how your family can help.

3. Decide on an activity that your family can do and do it! (An example might be donating clothes that children have outgrown to a group or agency that provides clothing for people in need.)

4. Talk about having a family project to help others every year.

Discussion Questions:

1. How would it feel to need help from the organization you are helping?

2.   What can we do in our family to help others?

3.   Why is it important to help other people?

Variation:

Assemble gift baskets with items families need. Purchase or design a container for your gifts. Decorate with a large bow and a handmade card that carries an appropriate message. Take the gift basket to an organization that will deliver it.

Adopt a Friend

Objective:

To care for someone who is lonely and to learn about the joy of doing things for someone else. (This is especially enjoyable for children whose grandparents live far away.)

Supplies Needed:

Depends on activity chosen.

Step-by-Step Instructions:

1.   Locate a person whose family is far away and who seldom has visitors. It may be someone in your neighborhood, at your church, synagogue or mosque or in a nursing home.

2.   Go as a family to meet the person and ask if your family can *adopt* her or him as a special person in your lives.

3.   Plan regular visits with your new friend. Consider reading a book together with the individual, sharing seasonal treats and/or watching a television special. Ask the person to share stories about her/his growing-up years, her/his family, where he/she lived as a child.

4.   If you like, make a scrapbook of the times you share together. Include pictures, stories, special cards and other keepsakes. Leave the scrapbook with your adopted friend occasionally so he/she can look at it and enjoy the memories it recalls.

Discussion Questions:

1. How would you feel if you lived alone or in a nursing home?

2. How would it be different if your family lived close by rather than far away?

3. What are some ways you can show your friend that you care for her/him?

Variation:

Contact a local nursing home and arrange for caroling. Make the event a tradition for your family.

Thanksgiving Prayer

Objective:

To create opportunities for intergenerational sharing and to develop an attitude of thankfulness.

Supplies Needed:

Pencil and paper.

Step-by-Step Instructions:

1. Choose an intergenerational committee to compose a special prayer for your family to share at Thanksgiving dinner. For generations-at-a-distance, this can be done via e-mail or by telephone.

2. Send a copy of the prayer home with each person.

3. Start a new family tradition by using this special prayer each year for Thanksgiving.

Variations:

Don't just be thankful at Thanksgiving! Occasionally, ask each person to share what they are thankful for before a family meal is served. Have each family member think of things they are thankful for. Together, write out the things each individual is thankful for with sidewalk chalk on the sidewalk. Each person will be reminded of what they are thankful for every time they come and go.

Discussion Questions:

1. Why is it important to remember why we are thankful?

2. How can we make being thankful more a part of our day-to-day lives?

3. How can family members show thankfulness to each other daily?

Alike or Different

Objective:

To help family members have respect for people of other ethnic groups, cultural groups or religions.

Supplies Needed:

None.

Step-by-Step Instructions:

1. When a situation comes up in the community, at school or on the news that highlights ethnic, cultural or religious issues, use this opportunity to talk with your family about what you believe or what appropriate reactions should be.

2. Use this framework to start your discussion:

   • What differences do you have compared with the person in question? Do these differences result in different values or ways of life?

   • How many ways are you similar to the person(s) in question? What might you do that is similar? What goals or interests might be alike?

   • How are your everyday activities the same? (What you eat; what you do, work/school; what you do after school or work; what clothes you wear.)

Discussion Questions:

1. Which are more important to focus on—similarities or differences?

2. Do differences in values or beliefs make another person less important or less deserving of respect?

3.   What do you think your life would be like if you were of a different ethnic or cultural group or religion? How would you feel if you were treated or talked about differently because of those differences?

Family Mission Statement

Objective:

As a couple, put together a statement of what your family wants to do, and to be in the future, and the principles that you choose to guide your family life.

Supplies Needed:

Pencil/pen and paper, plus poster-making supplies.

Step-by-Step Instructions:

1.   As a couple, sit down and consider questions like:

   • What is most important to us as a couple?

   • What are our priorities?

   • How do we want to relate to each other?

   • What are our responsibilities as family members?

2.   Make it fun! Brainstorm ideas. Get as many written down as you can. Then go back and pick out what's most important to you as a family.

3.   Make your mission statement short so everyone can remember it.

4.   When it's written, make a poster with your family mission statement on it. Post it someplace where you can see it every day.

Discussion Questions:

You have already considered several questions as you have written your family mission statement. Keep it where you can see it. Occasionally, talk about how your activities and choices are fitting into the mission statement you have written. If they are not compatible, you may want to reconsider what you are doing—or rewrite your mission statement.

1.   Did you post your family mission statement where you can see it every day?

2. How do your activities and choices fit into the statement?

3. What did you learn about other family members as you worked on the family mission statement?

Our Family Faith Scrapbook

Objective:

To emphasize the importance of your children and grandchildren knowing and understanding the principles of faith and/or the values that are the foundation of your family.

Supplies Needed:

Photos and album.

Step-by-Step Instructions:

1. Enlist your children's help. Decide which beliefs and values you want to include in your family faith scrapbook.

2. Find or take photos that illustrate each value or belief. Examples would be a photo of a baptism or a first communion to illustrate religious belief, or a photo of nature to illustrate your value of protecting the environment, along with journaling to explain why these are important.

3. You can designate one person as the writer or each family member can write their own feelings.

Discussion Questions:

1. How did you decide which beliefs and values to include?

2. How did you decide which photos to use?

3. Which photos need to be taken?

4. Why were some photos easier to find than others?

Spiritual Timeline

Objective:

To record steps in a family's spiritual timeline.

Supplies Needed:

Paper, colored pencils or pens.

Step-by-Step Instructions:

1. Each person should have a piece of paper and pencil/pen. Draw a line across the length of the paper to represent a person's lifetime. Start with birth on the left, marking years as you go across the page. (Youth will mark each year 1, 2, 3 and so forth; adults may want to mark time in five-or 10-year increments!)

2. Mark special events that you have experienced.

3. Ask the following discussion questions, adding markings for points on each spiritual timeline.

Discussion Questions:

1. What is your earliest memory of God?

2. What is your earliest memory or conversation about religion? How did you react?

3. What religious/spiritual event or experience stands out in your life?

4. When was your spiritual high point?

5. When was your spiritual low point?

6. Which special people have played a role in your spiritual journey?

7. Where would you like to go from here in your spiritual journey?

8. What steps do you need to take to get there?

Spiritual Workout

Objective:

To plan and carry out ways to grow spiritually as a family.

Supplies Needed:

Pencil and paper.

Step-by-Step Instructions:

1. Gather together as a family and talk about what you believe (your values) and how it influences the way you live.

2. Make a list together of ways you can be more effective in living your values. This list might include:

   - books you want to read individually or as a family that show the values that are important to you

   - attending religious services together

   - caring for someone who needs help

   - giving time or money to a charity

   - setting aside time to think and reflect alone

   - spending time appreciating nature together

   - volunteering in an important cause in which you believe

3. Set aside a specific time to do one of the things on your list.

Discussion Questions:

1. How did you feel about the activity?

2. Did it help strengthen your values? If yes, tell how it did. If no, how could we change it so it does make a difference?

3. What other things could we do as a family—or would you like to do individually—to express the things that are important? What could we do to grow spiritually?

4. Why do you think spiritual development is important to our overall develop-
    ment as a family?

5. Do you ever notice a difference between your talk and your walk? In other
    words, is there a difference between what you say you believe and what you
    actually do? How can each of us bring those two parts more into synchrony?

Tales of Courage

Objective:

To learn examples of people who persevered even when they were in difficult situations and to see how personal values have affected the choices made by people
throughout history.

Supplies Needed:

Books about historic figures. (These can be checked out from your local library.)

Step-by-Step Instructions:

1. Read a story together about someone who persevered when things were diffi-
    cult.

2. You may think of someone on your own. Here are some examples: Daniel,
    Esther, Joseph or Jonah in the Bible; Abraham Lincoln, Dr. Martin Luther
    King Jr., Amelia Earhart, Chief Joseph of the Nez Perce Indian tribe.

Discussion Questions:

1. What difficult decisions did the person have to make?

2. What standards or values influenced this person's decision?

3. What would people around this person have thought? Were their decisions
    popular?

4. How did the situation turn out?

5. What can I learn from their experience?

6. What book could we read next?

Square-Foot Scavenger Hunt

Objective:

To discover the details of creation.

Supplies Needed:

The out-of-doors, ruler, small flags/sticks. Optional: paper and pencil, magnifying glass.

Step-by-Step Instructions:

1. On a nice day for being out-of-doors, do a Square-Foot Scavenger Hunt with your family. Measure and mark off one square foot in the yard or park for each person participating. It may or may not be a place where you can dig in the dirt.

2. Get down on the ground and inspect each part of your area.

3. Either write down or remember each part of creation that you see: insects, plants, leaves, rocks, sticks, sand, etc. For even more detail, look through a magnifying glass.

Discussion Questions:

1. What different kinds of plants and insects did you see?

2. What do they need to live and grow?

3. How did they get there?

4. What else did you find? Did you find items that don't belong in nature? (Example: trash.)

5. In what ways do we take nature for granted?

6. What changes could we make as a family to improve our environment?

Share Your Change

Objective:

To help family members develop an attitude of sharing and caring.

Supplies Needed:

Container and change.

Step-by-Step Instructions:

1. As a family, talk about different groups or individuals who are in need in your religious group, neighborhood or community. Select one that you would like to help. Decorate a container (jar, can, box) for collecting change.

2. For the next month (or you designate the time period), ask each family member to put their change in the container every day.

3. At the end of your collection time, donate the money, along with a note of encouragement, to the needy person or group.

Discussion Questions:

1. How did it feel to share with others?

2. How did the other person or group respond?

3. In what other ways could you share with this person or group?

4. What project will you do the next time?

Enjoyable Time Together

Before reading the next section, think about the time you and your mate spend together. Also, think about the time your family spends together. Take the following assessment and discuss your responses to see how you are doing. Where would you like to see improvement? A planning guide is included so you can develop some goals. Use the activities at the end of this unit to help you. Enjoyable time together as a family and as a couple is time well-spent.

American Family Strengths Inventory©

Enjoyable Time Together

Family members can record their perceptions here in the area of *Enjoyable Time Together*. Feel free to make copies of this page for each member of your family, or there are additional copies of this Inventory in the Appendix. Once each member has completed the Inventory, record their responses on the Tally Sheet provided in the Appendix.

You may want to complete this survey now, then again in three months and again in another six months. That way, you can see how your family is progressing.

Put an "S" for *Strength* beside the qualities you feel your family has achieved and a "G" beside those qualities that are an area of potential *Growth*. If the particular characteristic does not apply to your family or is not a characteristic that is important to you, put an "NA" for *Not Applicable*. After recording your perceptions, spend some enjoyable time talking together about how your views are similar and how they are different.

Family Member's Name:_____ Date:_____

In Our Family ...

We have a number of common interests.   _____

We like to have fun together.   _____

We feel comfortable with each other.   _____

We enjoy trying out new activities together.   _____

We enjoy hearing our grandparents' stories about the past. _____

We enjoy simple, inexpensive family activities.   _____

We like to have a place we call home.   _____

We feel strongly connected with each other.   _____

Hanging out together builds strong relationships.   _____

We have lots of good times together.   _____

We often laugh with each other.   _____

Observing family rituals and customs is important to us. _____

We enjoy sharing our memories with each other. _____

We enjoy having unplanned, spontaneous activities with each other. _____

All things considered, we have adequate time for each other, and we enjoy the time we share together. _____

©Copyrighted material. For nonprofit educational purposes only. Not for resale.

Our Plan for Enjoyable Time Together

Now that you know your family's strengths related to enjoyable time together, read the next section. As you read, you may want to think about how the examples fit your family. You can then look at ways your family might enhance your time together and write them in the space below. The activities at the end of this section are there to help you get started.

Our Plan

Based on our family discussion about Enjoyable Time Together, *we have decided to do the following things in the coming weeks and months to enhance togetherness with each other.*

1. _____

_____

_____

_____

2. _____

_____

_____

_____

3. _____

_____

_____

_____

Signed: _____   _____

        _____   _____

        _____   _____

A Journey of Happy Memories

"Relax now. Close your eyes, and think back to when you were a child. Picture in your mind's eye a really good time you had as a kid. A really happy time. Go through several of these happy times until you come to the most memorable one of all. What was happening? Who were you with? Try to see it, hear it, touch it, taste it. When you open your eyes in a few minutes, we're going to ask you to describe this picture to everyone in the room."

The room gets very quiet. Some faces are lost in thought. Other faces have big smiles on them. After a sufficient amount of time, the group is asked to open their eyes.

"Now, let's have eight or nine people volunteer to come up front here. To tell us all, one by one, what they saw. What were these happy memories from childhood that you remember today, years later?"

This exercise has been done with literally thousands of people over the years, and their responses have been most instructive:

> I saw my father and me. I was sitting on his lap before bedtime. He was a busy man, working hard to support our family, but he always had time in the evening to read me a story. I loved the smell of his after-shave, and he always made me feel so safe and protected and we had fun laughing together.

> —

> Every Saturday morning my mom and I would scrub the kitchen floor together. We would get all sudsy and wet and laugh and tease each other and talk girl talk.

> —

> Thanksgiving was always so much fun. All the aunts and uncles and cousins would come to our house and we had an old pretty-much beat-up piano, and Mom would play and we would sing. But when the kids got tired of singing, we'd chase each other around the house and have fun giggling and running until the grown-ups sent us outside to run some more. It was great!

> —

> We would go camping at the same lake year after year. It was like an old friend. Money was pretty tight for Mom after Dad left, but she still figured out a way for us to go camping. I think she borrowed a tent from a neighbor

> and off we'd go. We'd swim and laugh and read grizzly bear stories at night and eat s'mores. I never wanted it to end.

———

> Grandpa would play checkers with me. Game after game after game. I was only seven or eight, and he'd never let me win. I think he wanted me to try harder and harder to get good, and so he would play hard, also, and I never won. But he had a way of not discouraging me by saying, "Good playing, Paulie! You almost did it! Let's try again." With my own kids, I let them win sometimes, and sometimes they even beat me legitimately. But the main thing is that we're together enjoying each other.

After listening to about a dozen stories of happy childhood memories, the audience is asked to work together to construct a Theory of Enjoyable Time Together. "What did you hear in these stories? What themes?"

First, the group concludes, happy childhood memories most commonly center on activities that are shared as a family. Simply being together and delighting in each other's company is the key. Second, pleasurable time together almost always focuses on activities that don't cost a lot of money. We like to call these *serendipitous good times* that occur when you're simply hanging out together, looking for ways to have fun together, and the creative genius of the family members becomes the catalyst for enjoyment.

The list of popular family activities that help cement the bonds of togetherness is a long one and includes: meals together, spending time outdoors in nature together, house and yard chores, attending sporting events, long quiet chats, board games and cards, and outdoor recreation, including camping, playing catch and other yard games, canoeing, hiking and picnicking. The particular activity isn't as important as the fact that the activity is a vehicle for human contact.

The Family That Eats Happily Together Stays Together

Mealtimes together can be especially good, and families that eat together a lot have countless opportunities to develop positive emotional bonds with each other. What good things happen when we break bread together? Here's what family members themselves have to say:

> We eat the evening meal together. In extreme cases, one of us may not be there, but everyone knows that being absent from dinner is not taken lightly.

We use that time to share triumphs and tribulations. In a hectic world we need some common ground where we can meet.

—

We always eat dinner together and try to be together for breakfast as well. And we have a rule of no television during meals.

—

It's a time when we can slow down, relax, and learn about all the ups and downs in each other's lives. Most of the times, the discussions are pretty relaxed. We make a big effort to be pleasant and build a positive atmosphere. Who wants indigestion? But, sometimes the discussions can focus on pretty serious issues, and after the food's all eaten, we'll still be sitting there trying to figure out how to meet one of life's challenges together.

—

When you've got little kids, mealtime can get pretty scary sometimes. We had one kid who would fall asleep in her spaghetti, nose down. We had another who liked to toss her food across the room. And sometimes the three of them would get in a raucous competition to see who could get the most attention from Mom and Dad. But most of the time it was a golden opportunity for us to hear good stories and witness the wonder of children's lives unfolding as they grew in the world. It was a sacred time.

A common mistake that many families make is to use mealtime as the means for correction ("Why didn't you do better on that math test?"), or nagging ("When are you going to clean your room?"). Children may also get in the habit of using this time to complain ("Everyone else gets to stay up late, why can't I?"). Setting mealtime ground rules can help. Discipline, complaining, fighting and arguing should not be a part of family meals. Instead, another time should be set aside to resolve these issues. Done the right way, family mealtime can be an enjoyable time for the family to be together.

Strengths-based Activities for Developing Enjoyable Time Together in the Family

Create a Holiday

Objective:

Create a holiday to establish traditions unique to you as a couple.

Supplies Needed:

Craft materials, decorations.

Step-by-Step Instructions:

1. Think about what kind of holiday would be of interest to both of you.

2. Discuss these questions together:

   - What food would be eaten during the holiday?
   - What activities would happen on this holiday?
   - What makes this day special and unique?
   - What sorts of decorations would be displayed during the holiday?
   - How often will the holiday happen—once a year, twice a year, etc.?
   - What day would work best so everyone can participate?

Discussion Questions:

1. What are some of the best parts of the holiday?

2. How will the holiday be celebrated in the future?

3. Are there other activities you can think of that would be unique to the two of you?

4. If you started a family, how would the new members fit into the holiday?

Variation:

If you have children, include them in designing a family holiday.

The Best Summer Ever

Objective:

To help couples plan for meaningful ways to spend time together during the summer (or anytime).

Supplies Needed:

Three pieces of poster board, colored markers, stickers, yardstick.

Step-by-Step Instructions:

1. Sometime during the spring, draw a calendar for the summer months, one month per sheet.

2. As a couple, talk about what would be the *perfect summer* for each person. Find out what is really important to each one. This is a time to think about being a *couple*. You can do this later with your family if you so desire.

3. You can't do everything, so decide how priorities will be determined: Is it by the time involved, cost, distance or another factor? Find a way for the decision-making process to be fair for each person.

4. Let each person put their activities on the calendar with a different colored marker. Use stickers to highlight special events. Don't fill every day—you need some room for flexibility!

5. Put the calendar in a place where both of you can see it regularly. Make adjustments as the summer progresses.

Discussion Questions:

1. What is really important to us as a couple?

2. How can we protect the time we have together?

3. Did each person get to do something that is special for her/him?

4. Did you have the *best summer ever*?

Variation:

If you have children, include them in the discussion and planning.

Family Get-Away

Objective:

To enjoy spending time together as a family.

Supplies Needed:

Cash, motel, stores.

Step-by-Step Instructions:

1. Select a specific time for your family to go shopping.

2. Staying overnight in a motel enables everyone to recover from the stress of shopping and enjoy the purchases made together. Note: There is no need to spend a lot of money. Window shopping can be just as much fun as buying! (For one family, the group shopping started with the need to purchase a prom dress but has continued each spring as a great way to get sisters and nieces together.)

Discussion Questions:

1. What did we learn about each other as a family?

2. What is the funniest thing that happened all day?

3. How does our family feel about spending money? Do we make lists of how much we'll spend? How do we make financial decisions?

4. What are other things we like to do as a family?

Getting Along

Objective:

To practice communicating with those you find difficult to get along with.

Supplies Needed:

A friend or family member who will role play with you.

Step-by-Step Instructions:

1. Think about people you know who are difficult to get along with.

2. Make a list and write down exactly why these people are hard to get along with. Think of ways in which you could modify your behavior/attitude toward them.

3. Ask a friend or family member (not the person you don't get along with!) to act in a similar fashion to the way the difficult person behaves. Role-play and try to practice new behavior/attitudes toward the difficult person.

4. Think of at least one nice thing you can do for someone who is hard to get along with.

Discussion Questions:

1. Why is it important to learn to get along well with others?

2. How should we deal with conflict in our own family?

3. How does your behavior influence how others behave?

4. How can you react in a positive way to someone who is difficult to get along with?

Family Scavenger Hunt

Objective:

To get family members of all ages working together with a common goal—having fun!

Supplies Needed:

Scavenger hunt clues, any special items needed to fulfill the tasks, bags for collecting the scavenged items.

Step-by-Step Instructions:

1. Develop questions of particular interest to your family. Questions may deal with some family history, such as: "Go to the spot where Grandpa asked Grandma to marry him, then get on your knees to find the next clue." (Hide the next clue under the couch, under a chair, etc.) You may have to ask Grandpa or Grandma where that spot might be, but what fun! Or, "Go to the room where most family meals are eaten."

2. Divide the family into two or more teams. Write the same questions on two or more different colored papers so each team will have its own color. Number the questions in a different order for each color.

3. Have the family teams search for clues for their team color only. Place questions and directions to find the next question in different locations. Use the entire house, yard or farm for your hunt. For example, have teams raid the refrigerator and have someone eat a dill pickle and ice cream or put a carton of eggs in the old chicken house and have one person eat an egg—hard-boiled of course, but don't tell them that! Look up Aunt Gertrude's phone number and write it down. Locate an ice scraper or sun screen. Have every group member make a basket with a basketball or jump rope five times.

4. End the hunt with the final clue for each team. For example, the final task may be a race around the house, pulling one or more team members in a wagon or running backward holding hands.

5. The number and type of questions can vary with how much space you have for the teams to use and your group. Some groups might even want teams to drive around the neighborhood, but include an *enforcer* to make sure seat-belts are always used and speed limits and laws are followed.

6. Make sure you plan enough time to set out the clues because it will take longer than you expect to get that done, but the family laughter is well worth the time spent on this project.

Discussion Questions:

1. What did you learn about your family?

2. What answers surprised you?

3.   What are other interesting things about your family?

4.   How can you help other family members learn about your family history?

Make a Natural Garland

Objective:

To make a seasonal decoration together or to provide food for birds.

Supplies Needed:

Blunt needles, coarse thread (or sewing thread doubled), cranberries, popcorn, cinnamon sticks, and so forth.

Step-by-Step Instructions:

1.   With a blunt needle and some coarse thread, string cranberries, popcorn and cinnamon sticks. (These are more economical if purchased in bulk, perhaps from a food co-op.) Popcorn may be difficult for young children because the kernels break easily.

2.   If using the garland as food for birds, watch to see what kinds of birds (or other wildlife) come to eat.

Discussion Questions:

1.   What kind of things would pioneer children have used to string a garland?

2.   What other things could you string that would be pretty—or that would provide food for birds?

3.   What was the most fun about working together as a family?

Pioneer Night

Objective:

To experience to some extent what it might have been like to be a pioneer family without our modern conveniences (i.e., electricity, microwave, telephone); and to spend time together without interruption.

Supplies Needed:

Fireplace, candles or oil lamps, food for a meal that can be cooked over a fire, a book to read aloud or games that might have been played by pioneer families, such as cards or checkers.

Step-by-Step Instructions:

1. Plan a supper in which the food can either be cooked over the fire or eaten as is.

2. Take the phone off the hook and turn off all the lights. Light candles or oil lamps for additional lighting. Be sure all candles or lamps are placed on non-flammable surfaces and away from curtains or other items that might easily catch fire. From this point on use nothing that requires electricity.

3. Prepare and eat the supper you have planned. (It may not be too authentic, but hot dogs and s'mores will do the trick. Add some fruit and raw vegetables, and water or milk to drink.)

4. After supper play cards or checkers or another game pioneer families might have played, or an adult or older child could read to the rest of the family.

Discussion Questions:

1. During the evening, discuss with the children what they think it would have been like to grow up in pioneer days. Ask questions such as: Where would your food come from? Where would you get water? How would you keep your house warm (or cool)? Where would you get your clothes? What do you think school would be like? What kind of toys do you think you would have? What other things do you think kids did to entertain themselves?

2. At the end of the evening, ask the children the following questions:

   - When did it seem to be the darkest, when we first turned out the lights or later in the evening?

   - What did we do differently because we did not use electricity?

   - Did not having electricity make things harder or easier?

   - Are there things we could do so we would not use as much electricity?

- What other games could we play together as a family (or what book would you like to read together)?

- What was your favorite part of the evening?

- What might we do if we planned another pioneer night or what else might we do together as a family?

A Family Movie

Objective:

Spend time together (away from the television).

Supplies Needed:

Story or idea, costumes, props and scenery, if desired. Videotape, if desired and if equipment is available.

Step-by-Step Instructions:

1. With your family decide on an idea for a movie you can create and star in. Think of television shows your family enjoys and rewrite them to fit your own family, or maybe a family member can write an original story. (Your child may have written one in school that would work very well.) A favorite child's book may also make a good movie.

2. You can write a script or do an impromptu show in your living room. Use your imagination for costumes, props and scenery.

3. After some practice, *stage* your performance. If you have a video recorder, invite a relative or friend to tape your family show.

Discussion Questions:

1. How does this compare with watching a show on television?

2. What makes a television show fun to watch? What are some problems with current television shows? What are some good things about current television shows?

3. What did you learn about each other during this activity?

4. How can acting be used in other ways with your family?

Variation:

Watch old family movies.

Your Family Value Culture

Objective:

Share information about your family's money culture to better understand your own money values.

Supplies Needed:

None.

Step-by-Step Instructions:

1. Designate an uninterrupted time for your family to talk about values, especially those related to money. The following questions can be used as a guide:

    *   Should money be saved or spent?

    *   How much money is *a lot* of money?

    *   What would happen if we had less money than we do now?

    *   If you could choose between getting a million dollars or spending an entire week with your family, which would you choose? Why?

2. Discuss other questions as they arise. If you have teenagers, think about what they might need to know about becoming financially independent. If you have younger children, talk about how money is earned in the family and how financial decisions are made.

3. Copy the following sayings onto slips of paper. Cut them apart and put them in a jar. Ask each family member to draw out a slip of paper and tell what he/she thinks the saying means.

    You know, money doesn't grow on trees.

    A penny saved is a penny earned.

Don't spend it all in one place.

Easy come; easy go.

Do you think I'm made of money?

There is no free lunch.

He's only out for the money.

It is better to give than to receive.

Neither a borrower nor a lender be.

The love of money is the root of all evil.

Discussion Questions:

Discuss the various sayings you hear family members make about money. Talk about the following questions:

1. Who says what about money in our family?

2. What do they mean?

3. How does it make you feel?

4. What sayings about money have you heard on TV and in the movies?

5. What was your reaction?

6. How do you think these have influenced your own money values?

7. What did you learn about your family?

8. What values influence how your family spends money?

Owl Moon Walk

Objective:

To experience the wonders of life as a family.

Supplies needed:

A moonlit night, the book *Owl Moon* by Jane Yolen and John Schoenherr, snow (optional).

Step-by-Step Instructions:

1. Read *Owl Moon*. (If you cannot get the book, don't worry, you can still do the rest!)

2. On a moonlit, snowy night, take a walk to hear the owls. It does not matter if you don't actually hear owls.

3. Listen to the snow squeaking as you walk.

4. Whisper.

5. Find joy in each other.

Discussion Questions:

1. What did you discover on your walk? (Did you see your breath, hear the sound of the snow, see the stars, see the moon? Describe what it was like being together, etc.).

2. What did you like most about your walk?

3. What are some other things in nature you would like to experience?

Remember, don't get so wrapped up in making it meaningful that you forget to just enjoy.

Variation:

What other books could you read?

Global Measures of the Family's Strengths

In Our Family ...

We love one another.   _____

Life in our family is satisfying to us.   _____

We are a happy family.   _____

All things considered, we are a strong family.   _____

©Copyrighted material. For nonprofit educational purposes only. Not for resale.

Appendix

More About Couple and Family Strengths Research

Research on successful families can be traced back in the literature to at least the beginning of the Great Depression in the United States (Woodhouse, 1930). Fascination with a focus on family problems, however, has always dominated researchers' thinking. When Herbert Otto began his work on strong families and family strengths in the early 1960s, it became readily apparent that problems had proven far more interesting than strengths to a wide variety of professions (Gabler & Otto, 1964; Otto, 1962, 1963).

Family strengths did not capture much interest again until Nick Stinnett began his work at Oklahoma State University in 1974 and moved to the University of Nebraska in 1977. Stinnett, DeFrain and their colleagues then began publishing a continuous series of articles and books (Casas, Stinnett, Williams, DeFrain & Lee, 1984; DeFrain, DeFrain, & Lepard, 1994; DeFrain & Stinnett, 2002; Olson & DeFrain, 2006; Stinnett & DeFrain, 1985; Stinnett & O'Donnell, 1996; Stinnett & Sauer, 1977; Xie, DeFrain, Meredith & Combs, 1996).

A series of family strengths conferences beginning in 1978 proved to be a catalyst for research on strong families. Nine volumes of proceedings were published as a result of the National Symposium on Building Family Strengths series (Stinnett, Chesser, & DeFrain, 1979; Stinnett, Chesser, DeFrain & Knaub, 1980; Stinnett, DeFrain, et al., 1981; Stinnett, DeFrain, et. al., 1982; Rowe, DeFrain, et. al., 1984; Williams, Lingren, et. al., 1985; VanZandt, Lingren, et. al., 1986; Lingren, Kimmons, et. al., 1988).

An International Family Strengths Network (IFSN) began working on a series of family strengths gatherings in the late 1990s, and to date there have been more than 30 conferences held in North America, Asia and Australia. Upcoming events are planned for Africa, the Middle East and Europe. International Family and Culture Study Tours are regularly linked to these gatherings, so that participants have a chance to discuss family issues with colleagues and then stay with local families and visit historic and cultural sites important to families. The IFSN is an informal collection of colleagues and friends around the world; there are no dues and, in the words of the KwaZulu Natal in South Africa, together we create "something out of nothing."

These conferences create a synergy that sparks research, policy and educational activities on behalf of millions of families around the world, and remind the participants that in the final analysis, people are people are people and families are families are families. Recent research and education projects have begun in the People's Republic of China, Australia, Mexico and the Republic of Korea as a result of these conferences.

Family strengths studies using the family strengths model have been conducted in 28 countries: Argentina, Australia, Austria, Brazil, Canada, Chile, Colombia, Ecuador, Fiji, Germany, India, Iraq, Korea, Mexico, New Zealand, Pakistan, Panama, Peru, Romania, Russia, Somalia, South Africa, Switzerland, Thailand, Ukraine, United Arab Emirates, U.S.A. and Venezuela. Some of these research projects have been much more extensive than others, and, in every country, there is always room for new, creative studies.

The cutting edge for family strengths research today is in two broad areas: continued work on family strengths studies in myriad cultures around the world; and research on how findings of these studies can be applied to everyday life—applied in educational settings, programs and materials for families; applied in family therapy; and applied by governments in developing family-strengthening policies and initiatives. A number of colleagues in the International Family Strengths Network can be tapped for help and are very open to joint national and international efforts for strengthening families. For more information, feel free to e-mail John DeFrain: jdefrain1@unl.edu. We are happy to share research instruments and other materials at no cost, and we regularly update our Web site: unlforfamilies@unl.edu.

Prominent Research Efforts

When Otto catalogued research on family strengths in the 1960s, he found allusions to success scattered broadly across many fields and innumerable terms for describing healthy behaviors in families. His literature review, looking at studies between the late 1940s and early 1960s noted that researchers used 515 different terms to describe healthy behaviors in families (Gabler & Otto, 1964; Otto, 1964; Otto, 1962).

We have chosen to use the terms strong families, strong marriages, couple strengths and family strengths in our studies over the years. These terms are readily understandable to a broad spectrum of people attending educational programming that focuses on strengthening families. Other investigators have used a variety of terms, including strong family, happy family, good family, healthy family, successful family, resilient family, balanced family, optimally-functioning family and so forth. While terminology may differ considerably, the basic concepts used in the various models from researcher to researcher are remarkably similar. This can be readily seen when examining some of the key theorists interested in healthy functioning families as noted in the table following.

Dimensions of Family Strength as Delineated By Prominent Researchers

Theorists and Countries	Dimensions
Beavers and Hampson (1990). U.S.A.	Centripetal/centrifugal interaction, closeness, parent coalitions, autonomy, adaptability, egalitarian power, goal-directed negotiation, ability to resolve conflict, clarity of expression, range of feelings, openness to others, empathic understanding
Billingsley (1986). U.S.A.	Strong family ties, strong religious orientation, educational aspirations/achievements
Curran (1983). U.S.A.	Togetherness, respect and trust, shared leisure, privacy valued, shared mealtime, shared responsibility, family rituals, communication, affirmation of each other, religious love, humor/play
Epstein, Bishop, Ryan, Miller, and Keitner (1993). Canada.	Affective involvement, behavior control, communication
Geggie, DeFrain, Hitchcock and Silberberg (2000). Australia.	Communication (open, positive, honest, including humor), togetherness, sharing activities, affection, support, acceptance, commitment, resilience
Kantor and Lehr (1974). U.S.A.	Affect, power
Krysan, Moore and Zill (1990). U.S.A.	Commitment to family, time together, encouragement of individuals, ability to adapt, clear roles, communication, religious orientation, social connectedness

Mberengwa and Johnson (2003). Botswana.	Consensus as a means of settling differences, anger management, concern for the welfare of one's kin, valuing their culture, respect toward others, *kgotla* (community development associations) for strengthening neighborhoods
Olson, McCubbin, Barnes, Larsen, Muxen, and Wilson (1989); Olson and Olson (2000). U.S.A.	Strong marriage, high family cohesion, good family flexibility, effective coping with stress and crisis, positive couple and family communication
Otto (1962, 1963); Gabler and Otto (1964). U.S.A.	Shared religious and moral values; love, consideration and understanding; common interests, goals and purposes; love and happiness of children; working and playing together; sharing specific recreational activities
D. Reiss (1981). U.S.A.	Coordination, closure
Sani and Buhannad (2003). United Arab Emirates.	Patriarchal family structure; family-arranged marriages; gender-based rights, responsibilities and privileges; strong emotional family bonds (*muwada*); extended family (*dhurriyah*); living with or next extended family members; frequent consultation; elders as role models and advisors; crises are tests from Allah; Islamic beliefs (*taqwa*) and practices provide optimal guidelines; collectivism over individualism; the government is supportive of individual, couple and family well-being
Stinnett, DeFrain and their colleagues (1977, 1985, 2002). U.S.A.	Appreciation and affection, commitment, positive communication, enjoyable time together, spiritual well-being, effective management of stress and crisis
Xia, Xie, and Zhou (2004); Xie, DeFrain, Meredith, and Combs (1996); Xu and Ye. (2002). China.	Togetherness and time together across three generations; love, care and commitment; communication; family support; spirituality (at peace with nature, at peace with oneself, at peace with others, at peace with the world); family oriented and harmonious
Yoo (2004); Yoo, DeFrain, Lee, Kim, Hong, Choi and Ahn (2004). Korea.	Respect, commitment, appreciation and affection, positive communication, sharing values and goals, role performing, physical health, connectedness with social systems, economic stability, ability to solve problems

The International Family Strengths Perspective

This perspective or conceptual framework is presented in more detail in the first section of this book. We present it one more time in abbreviated form, and encourage family educators to run off copies and use it for discussion purposes in your classes with family members, and in classes for individuals training to be professionals in the field of family life education and related disciplines.

The International Family Strengths Perspective

- *Families, in all their remarkable diversity, are the basic foundation of human cultures.*

- *All families have strengths.* And, all families have challenges and areas of potential growth.

- *If one looks only for problems in a family, one will see only problems.* If one also looks for strengths, one will find strengths.

- *It's not about structure, it's about function.* There are strong single-parent families, strong stepfamilies, strong nuclear families, strong extended families, strong families with gay and lesbian members and strong two-parent families.

- *Strong marriages are the center of many strong families.* The couple relationship is an important source of strength in many families with children who are doing well.

- *Strong families tend to produce great kids; and a good place to look for great kids is in strong families.*

- *If you grew up in a strong family as a child, it will probably be easier for you to create a strong family of your own as an adult.* But, it's also quite possible to do so if you weren't so lucky and grew up in a seriously troubled family.

- *The relationship between money and family strengths is shaky, at best.* Once a family has adequate financial resources—and *adequate* is a slippery and subjective word to define—the relentless quest for more and more money is not likely to increase the family's quality of life, happiness together or the strength of their relationships with each other. "The best things in life are not things."

- *Strengths develop over time.* When couples start out in life together, they sometimes have considerable difficulty adjusting to each other, and these difficulties are quite predictable.

- *Strengths are often developed in response to challenges.* A couple and family's strengths are tested by life's everyday stressors and also by the significant crises that all of us face sooner or later.

- *Strong families don't tend to think much about their strengths, they just live them.*

- *Strong families, like people, are not perfect.* A strong family is a piece of art continually in progress, always in the process of growing.

- *When seeking to unite groups of people, communities, and even nations, uniting around the cause of strengthening families—a cause we can all sanction—can be a powerful strategy.*

- *Human beings have the right and responsibility to feel safe, comfortable, happy and loved.* Strong families are where this all happens.

Adapted from: DeFrain, J., & Stinnett, N. (2002). Family strengths. In J.J. Ponzetti et al. (Eds.), *International encyclopedia of marriage and family* (2nd ed.). New York: Macmillan Reference Group, 637-642.

American Family Strengths Inventory— *for Professional Use*

Some readers who work with families will find it useful to have complete copies of the American Family Strengths Inventory (AFSI). While the Inventory appears earlier in this book broken down into separate components, professional educators might find it helpful for use with families in its entirety. For example, audiences can fill out the AFSI one strength at a time, discussing what they are finding about themselves and their family with the group facilitator moderating the discussion. This can be a very worthwhile activity lasting an hour and a half or more. (An audience usually can get through only three or four strengths in this time frame, and will have to fill out the rest of the AFSI and discuss it together at home.) Or, the AFSI can be used to introduce each of the strengths one at a time in a six-week workshop setting, each meeting lasting a couple hours. Use your creative gifts as you design ways the AFSI can be used as a tool to help families understand themselves better.

We are sharing this instrument with the reader because we want to see the AFSI used widely. There are three stipulations: 1) that it not be used for profit; 2) that you honor our copyright to the material and keep our names on it; and 3) that you, in turn, share the results of your work with us so that we can learn from you, just as you have learned from us. This reciprocal learning process will help advance family strengths-based work around the world.

Please keep in contact about your experiences with the AFSI and other family strengths-related matters by e-mailing John DeFrain: jdefrain1@unl.edu.

The American Family Strengths Inventory

A Teaching Tool for Generating Discussion on the Qualities that Make a Family Strong

Researchers: John DeFrain, Ph.D., Professor   Nick Stinnett, Ph.D., Professor
                Extension Family and Community   Department of Human Development
                Development Specialist   and Family Studies
                University of Nebraska–Lincoln   University of Alabama
                Lincoln, Nebraska 68583-0801   Tuscaloosa, Alabama
                Phone: (402) 472-1659   Phone: (205) 348-7864
                E-mail: jdefrain1@unl.edu   E-mail: nstinne1@ches.ua.edu

Research in the United States and around the world has found that strong families have a wide variety of qualities that contribute to the family members' sense of personal worth and feelings of satisfaction in their relationships with each other. A first step in developing the strengths of one's family is to assess those areas in which the family is doing well, and those areas in which family members would like to grow further.

The qualities of strong families in America can be broken down into six general categories, as outlined in the following pages. Put an "S" for Strength beside the qualities you feel your family has achieved, and a "G" beside those qualities that are an area of potential Growth. If the particular characteristic does not apply to your family or is not a characteristic important to you, put an "NA" for Not Applicable.

By doing this exercise, family members will be able to identify those areas they would like to work on together to improve, and those areas of strength that will serve as the foundation for their growth and positive change together.

This American Family Strengths Inventory has been validated through research with more than 24,000 family members in the United States and 27 other countries around the world. These studies of family strengths have been conducted by Nick Stinnett, John DeFrain and their colleagues since 1974.

For more information about this research, see:

DeFrain, J. (1999). Strong families around the world. *Family Matters: Australian Institute of Family Studies, 53* (Winter), 6-13.

DeFrain, J., Cook, R., & Gonzalez-Kruger, G. (2005). Family health and dysfunction. In R.J. Coombs (Ed.), *Family Therapy Review*. Mahwah, NJ: Lawrence Erlbaum Associates, 3-20.

DeFrain, J., & Stinnett, N. (2002). Family strengths. In J.J. Ponzetti et al. (Eds.), *International encyclopedia of marriage and family* (2nd ed.). New York: Macmillan Reference Group, 637-642.

Olson, D.H., & DeFrain, J. (2006). *Marriages and families: Intimacy, diversity, and strengths*, 5th ed. Boston: McGraw-Hill.

Stinnett, N., & DeFrain, J. (1985). *Secrets of strong families*. Boston: Little, Brown.

Appreciation and Affection for Each Other

In Our Family …

We appreciate each other and let each other know this. _____

We enjoy helping each other. _____

We are good at keeping our promises to each other. _____

We like to show affection to each other. _____

We feel close to each other. _____

We like to be kind to each other. _____

We like to hug each other. _____

We enjoy being thoughtful toward each other. _____

We wait for each other without complaining. _____

We give each other enough time to complete necessary tasks. _____

We grow stronger because we love each other. _____

All things considered, we have appreciation and affection for each other. _____

©Copyrighted material. For nonprofit educational purposes only. Not for resale.

Commitment to Each Other

In Our Family …

Responsibilities are shared fairly. _____

Everyone gets a say in making decisions. _____

Individuals are allowed to make their own choices and encouraged to take responsibility for these choices. _____

We find it easy to trust each other. _____

We like to do things for each other that make us feel good about ourselves. _____

We have reasonable expectations for each other. _____

We allow each other to be ourselves. _____

We have a high regard for each other. _____

We respect the roles each of us plays in the family. _____

We find it easy to be honest with each other. _____

We accept that each of us has different ways of doing things. _____

We build each other's self-esteem. _____

All things considered, we value each other and are committed to our well-being as a family. _____

©Copyrighted material. For nonprofit educational purposes only. Not for resale.

Positive Communication

In Our Family ...

We feel comfortable sharing our feelings with each other. _____

It is easy to understand each other's feelings. _____

We like to talk openly with each other. _____

We like to listen to each other. _____

We respect each other's point of view. _____

Talking through issues is important to us. _____

We give each other a chance to explain ourselves. _____

We enjoy our family discussions. _____

We share funny stories together. _____

Putdowns are rare. _____

Sarcasm is not generally used. _____

All things considered, communication in our family is positive and effective. _____

©Copyrighted material. For nonprofit educational purposes only. Not for resale.

Managing Stress and Crisis Effectively

In Our Family ...

A crisis has helped us grow closer together. _____

It is easy to find solutions to our problems when we talk about them. _____

It's important to try to change the things that we agree need changing, rather than ignoring the situation. _____

We can work together to solve very difficult family problems. _____

A crisis helps make our relationship strong. _____

We try not to worry too much because things usually work out OK. _____

We are able to face daily issues confidently. _____

We like to support each other. _____

Our friends are there when we need them. _____

A crisis makes us stick closer together. _____

We always find something good comes from a crisis. _____

We find it easy to make changes in our plans to meet changing circumstances. _____

We have the courage to try to do new things in life that will improve things for our family. _____

We can accept things in life that we know cannot be changed and find peace. _____

All things considered, we look at challenges as opportunities for growth. _____

©Copyrighted material. For nonprofit educational purposes only. Not for resale.

Spiritual Well-being

In Our Family ...

We have a hopeful attitude toward life. _____

Our home feels like a sanctuary to all of us. _____

We have a strong sense of belonging. _____

We enjoy learning about our family history. _____

We feel strong connections with our ancestors. _____

There is a feeling of safety and security. _____

We feel connected with nature and the world around us. _____

We feel a strong connection with the land. _____

There is a sense of peace among us. _____

We believe that love is a powerful force that keeps us together. _____

We benefit in many ways from our belief in a higher being or power. _____

It is easy to share our spiritual values and beliefs with each other. _____

Our personal religious beliefs are compatible with each other. _____

All things considered, we have strong spiritual connections that enhance our well-being. _____

©Copyrighted material. For nonprofit educational purposes only. Not for resale.

Enjoyable Time Together

In Our Family ...

We have a number of common interests. _____

We like to have fun together. _____

We feel comfortable with each other. _____

We enjoy trying out new activities together. _____

We enjoy hearing our grandparents' stories about the past. _____

We enjoy simple, inexpensive family activities. _____

We like to have a place we call home. _____

We feel strongly connected to each other. _____

Hanging out together builds strong relationships. _____

We have lots of good times together. _____

We often laugh with each other. _____

Observing family rituals and customs is important to us. _____

We enjoy sharing our memories with each other. _____

We enjoy having unplanned, spontaneous activities with each other. _____

All things considered, we have adequate time for each other, and we enjoy the time we share together. _____

©Copyrighted material. For nonprofit educational purposes only. Not for resale.

Global Measures of the Family's Strengths

In Our Family ...

We love one another. _____

Life in our family is satisfying to us. _____

We are a happy family. _____

All things considered, we are a strong family. _____

©Copyrighted material. For nonprofit educational purposes only. Not for resale.

American Family Strengths Inventory—
Individual Family Strengths Sheets

American Family Strengths Inventory©
Appreciation and Affection for Each Other

Family members can record their perceptions here in the area of *Appreciation and Affection for Each Other*. Feel free to make copies of this for each member of your family. Once each member has completed the Inventory, record their responses on the Composite sheet. Make additional copies as needed. You may want to complete this survey now, then again in three months and again in another six months. That way, you can see how your family is progressing.

Put an "S" for Strength beside the qualities you feel your family has achieved and a "G" beside those qualities that are an area of potential Growth. If the particular characteristic does not apply to your family or is not a characteristic that is important to you, put an "NA" for Not Applicable.

After recording your perceptions, spend some enjoyable time talking together about how your views are similar and how they are different. Remember: No one is absolutely right and no one is absolutely wrong on this. Everyone has a valid perception of what is happening and their views need to be considered carefully and respectfully.

Family Member's Name:_____ Date:_____

In Our Family ...

We appreciate each other and let each other know this.   _____

We enjoy helping each other.   _____

We are good at keeping our promises to each other.   _____

We like to show affection to each other.   _____

We feel close to each other.   _____

We like to be kind to each other.   _____

We like to hug each other.   _____

We enjoy being thoughtful toward each other.   _____

We wait for each other without complaining.   _____

We give each other enough time to complete necessary tasks.   _____

We grow stronger because we love each other.   _____

All things considered, we have appreciation and affection for each other.   _____

©Copyrighted material. For nonprofit educational purposes only. Not for resale.

American Family Strengths Inventory©

Commitment to Each Other

Family members can record their perceptions here in the area of *Commitment to Each Other*. Feel free to make copies of this for each member of your family. Once each member has completed the Inventory, record their responses on the Composite sheet. You may want to complete this survey now, then again in three months and again in another six months. That way, you can see how your family is progressing.

Put an "S" for Strength beside the qualities you feel your family has achieved and a "G" beside those qualities that are an area of potential Growth. If the particular characteristic does not apply to your family or is not a characteristic that is important to you, put an "NA" for Not Applicable.

After recording your perceptions, spend some enjoyable time talking together about how your views are similar and how they are different. Remember: No one is absolutely right and no one is absolutely wrong on this. Everyone has a valid perception of what is happening and their views need to be considered carefully and respectfully. If you see ways to work together to enhance your strengths in the area of *Commitment to Each Other*, feel free to jump in and do so in the coming days and weeks.

Family Member's Name:_____ Date:_____

In Our Family ...

Responsibilities are shared fairly. _____

Everyone gets a say in making decisions. _____

Individuals are allowed to make their own choices and encouraged to take responsibility for these choices. _____

We find it easy to trust each other. _____

We like to do things for each other that make us feel good about ourselves. _____

We have reasonable expectations for each other. _____

We allow each other to be ourselves. _____

We have a high regard for each other. _____

We respect the roles each of us plays in the family.   _____

We find it easy to be honest with each other.   _____

We accept that each of us has different ways of doing things.   _____

We build each other's self-esteem.   _____

All things considered, we value each other and are committed to our well-being as a family.   _____

©Copyrighted material. For nonprofit educational purposes only. Not for resale.

American Family Strengths Inventory©

Positive Communication

Family members can record their perceptions here in the area of *Positive Communication*. Feel free to make copies of this for each member of your family. Once each member has completed the Inventory, record their responses on the Composite sheet. You may want to complete this survey now, then again in three months and again in another six months. That way, you can see how your family is progressing.

Put an "S" for Strength beside the qualities you feel your family has achieved and a "G" beside those qualities that are an area of potential Growth. If the particular characteristic does not apply to your family or is not a characteristic that is important to you, put an "NA" for Not Applicable.

After recording your perceptions, spend some enjoyable time talking together about how your views are similar and how they are different. Remember: No one is absolutely right and no one is absolutely wrong on this. Everyone has a valid perception of what is happening and their views need to be considered carefully and respectfully. If you see ways to work together to enhance your strengths in the area of *Positive Communication*, feel free to jump in and do so in the coming days and weeks.

Family Member's Name:_____ Date:_____

In Our Family ...

We feel comfortable sharing our feelings with each other. _____

It is easy to understand each other's feelings. _____

We like to talk openly with each other. _____

We like to listen to each other. _____

We respect each other's point of view. _____

Talking through issues is important to us. _____

We give each other a chance to explain ourselves. _____

We enjoy our family discussions. _____

We share funny stories together. _____

Putdowns are rare.   _____

Sarcasm is not generally used.   _____

All things considered, communication in our family is positive and effective.   _____

©Copyrighted material. For nonprofit educational purposes only. Not for resale.

American Family Strengths Inventory©

Managing Stress and Crisis Effectively

Family members can record their perceptions here in the area of *Managing Stress and Crisis Effectively*. Feel free to make copies of this for each member of your family. Once each member has completed the Inventory, record their responses on the Composite sheet. You may want to complete this survey now, then again in three months and again in another six months. That way, you can see how your family is progressing.

Put an "S" for Strength beside the qualities you feel your family has achieved and a "G" beside those qualities that are an area of potential Growth. If the particular characteristic does not apply to your family or is not a characteristic that is important to you, put an "NA" for Not Applicable. After recording your perceptions, spend some enjoyable time talking together about how your views are similar and how they are different.

Family Member's Name:_____ Date:_____

In Our Family ...

A crisis has helped us grow closer together. _____

It is easy to find solutions to our problems when we talk about them. _____

It's important to try to change the things that we agree need changing, rather than ignoring the situation. _____

We can work together to solve very difficult family problems. _____

A crisis helps make our relationships strong. _____

We try not to worry too much because things usually work out OK. _____

We are able to face daily issues confidently. _____

We like to support each other. _____

Our friends are there when we need them. _____

A crisis makes us stick closer together. _____

We always find something good comes from a crisis. _____

We find it easy to make changes in our plans to meet changing circumstances. _____

We have the courage to try to do new things in life that will improve things for our family.   _____

We can accept things in life that we know cannot be changed and find peace.   _____

All things considered, we look at challenges as opportunities for growth.   _____

©Copyrighted material. For nonprofit educational purposes only. Not for resale.

American Family Strengths Inventory©

Spiritual Well-being

Family members can record their perceptions here in the area of *Spiritual Well-being*. Feel free to make copies of this for each member of your family. Once each member has completed the Inventory, record their responses on the Composite sheet. You may want to complete this survey now, then again in three months and again in another six months. That way, you can see how your family is progressing.

Put an "S" for Strength beside the qualities you feel your family has achieved and a "G" beside those qualities that are an area of potential Growth. If the particular characteristic does not apply to your family or is not a characteristic that is important to you, put an "NA" for Not Applicable. After recording your perceptions, spend some enjoyable time talking together about how your views are similar and how they are different.

Family Member's Name:_____ Date:_____

In Our Family ...

We have a hopeful attitude toward life. _____

Our home feels like a sanctuary to all of us. _____

We have a strong sense of belonging. _____

We enjoy learning about our family history. _____

We feel strong connections with our ancestors. _____

There is a feeling of safety and security. _____

We feel connected with nature and the world around us. _____

We feel a strong connection with the land. _____

There is a sense of peace among us. _____

We believe that love is a powerful force that keeps us together. _____

We benefit in many ways from our belief in a higher being or power. _____

It is easy to share our spiritual values and beliefs with each other. _____

Our personal religious beliefs are compatible with each other.   _____

All things considered, we have strong spiritual connections that enhance our well-being.   _____

©Copyrighted material. For nonprofit educational purposes only. Not for resale.

American Family Strengths Inventory©

Enjoyable Time Together

Family members can record their perceptions here in the area of *Enjoyable Time Together*. Feel free to make copies of this for each member of your family. Once each member has completed the Inventory, record their responses on the Composite sheet. You may want to complete this survey now, then again in three months and again in another six months. That way, you can see how your family is progressing.

Put an "S" for Strength beside the qualities you feel your family has achieved and a "G" beside those qualities that are an area of potential Growth. If the particular characteristic does not apply to your family or is not a characteristic that is important to you, put an "NA" for Not Applicable. After recording your perceptions, spend some enjoyable time talking together about how your views are similar and how they are different.

Family Member's Name:_____ Date:_____

In Our Family ...

We have a number of common interests. _____

We like to have fun together. _____

We feel comfortable with each other. _____

We enjoy trying out new activities together. _____

We enjoy hearing our grandparents' stories about the past. _____

We enjoy simple, inexpensive family activities. _____

We like to have a place we call home. _____

We feel strongly connected to each other. _____

Hanging out together builds strong relationships. _____

We have lots of good times together. _____

We often laugh with each other. _____

Observing family rituals and customs is important to us. _____

We enjoy sharing our memories with each other. _____

We enjoy having unplanned, spontaneous activities with each other. _____

All things considered, we have adequate time for each other, and we enjoy the time we share together. _____

©Copyrighted material. For nonprofit educational purposes only. Not for resale.

Global Measures of the Family's Strengths

In Our Family ...

We love one another. _____

Life in our family is satisfying to us. _____

We are a happy family. _____

All things considered, we are a strong family. _____

©Copyrighted material. For nonprofit educational purposes only. Not for resale.

American Family Strengths Inventory—
Composite Family Strengths Sheets

Ideally, each family member capable of doing so will fill out an individual American Family Strengths Inventory for each of the family strengths. Then, everyone's individual responses can be transferred to the Composite Family Strengths sheets on pages 178 to 188.

When you have done this, you are ready to have a wonderful family discussion focusing on ways your family is strong.

American Family Strengths Inventory©

Appreciation and Affection for Each Other—Composite

After all family members have filled out their individual American Family Strengths Inventories, you then can transfer each person's responses on *Appreciation and Affection for Each Other* to this Composite form.

After recording your perceptions, spend some enjoyable time talking together about how your views are similar and how they are different. Remember: No one is absolutely right and no one is absolutely wrong on this. Everyone has a valid perception of what is happening and their views need to be considered carefully and respectfully.

Date:_____   **Family Members' Names**

In Our Family ...   ____   ____   ____   ____

We appreciate each other and let each other   ____   ____   ____   ____
know this.

We enjoy helping each other.   ____   ____   ____   ____

We are good at keeping our promises to
each other.   ____   ____   ____   ____

We like to show affection to each other.   ____   ____   ____   ____

We feel close to each other.   ____   ____   ____   ____

We like to be kind to each other.   ____   ____   ____   ____

We like to hug each other.   ____   ____   ____   ____

We enjoy being thoughtful toward each other.   ____   ____   ____   ____

We wait for each other without complaining.   ____   ____   ____   ____

We give each other enough time to complete
necessary tasks.   ____   ____   ____   ____

We grow stronger because we love each
other.   ____   ____   ____   ____

*All things considered, we have appreciation
and affection for each other.*   ____   ____   ____   ____

©Copyrighted material. For nonprofit educational purposes only. Not for resale.

American Family Strengths Inventory©

Commitment to Each Other—Composite

After all family members have filled out their individual American Family Strengths Inventories, you then can transfer each person's responses on *Commitment to Each Other* to this Composite form.

After recording your perceptions, spend some enjoyable time talking together about how your views are similar and how they are different. Remember: No one is absolutely right and no one is absolutely wrong on this. Everyone has a valid perception of what is happening and their views need to be considered carefully and respectfully. If you see ways to work together to enhance your strengths in the area of *Commitment to Each Other*, feel free to jump in and do so in the coming days and weeks.

Date:_____   **Family Members' Names**

In Our Family ...   ____   ____   ____   ____

    Responsibilities are shared fairly.   ____   ____   ____   ____

    Everyone gets a say in making decisions.   ____   ____   ____   ____

    Individuals are allowed to make their own choices and encouraged to take responsibility for these choices.   ____   ____   ____   ____

    We find it easy to trust each other.   ____   ____   ____   ____

    We like to do things for each other that make us feel good about ourselves.   ____   ____   ____   ____

    We have reasonable expectations for each other.   ____   ____   ____   ____

    We allow each other to be herself/himself.   ____   ____   ____   ____

    We have a high regard for each other.   ____   ____   ____   ____

    We respect the roles each of us plays in the family.   ____   ____   ____   ____

    We find it easy to be honest with each other.   ____   ____   ____   ____

    We accept that each of us has different ways of doing things.   ____   ____   ____   ____

We build each other's self esteem.   ____   ____   ____   ____

*All things considered, we value each other
and are committed to our well-being as a
family.*   ____   ____   ____   ____

©Copyrighted material. For nonprofit educational purposes only. Not for resale.

American Family Strengths Inventory©

Positive Communication—Composite

After all family members have filled out their individual American Family Strengths Inventories, you then can transfer each person's responses on *Positive Communication* to this Composite form.

After recording your perceptions, spend some enjoyable time talking together about how your views are similar and how they are different. Remember: No one is absolutely right and no one is absolutely wrong on this. Everyone has a valid perception of what is happening and their views need to be considered carefully and respectfully.

Date:_____   **Family Members' Names**

In Our Family ...   ____   ____   ____   ____

We feel comfortable sharing our feelings with each other.	____	____	____	____
It is easy to understand each other's feelings.	____	____	____	____
We like to talk openly with each other.	____	____	____	____
We like to listen to each other.	____	____	____	____
We respect each other's point of view.	____	____	____	____
Talking through issues is important to us.	____	____	____	____
We give each other a chance to explain ourselves.	____	____	____	____
We enjoy our family discussions.	____	____	____	____
We share funny stories together.	____	____	____	____
Putdowns are rare.	____	____	____	____
Sarcasm is not generally used.	____	____	____	____
All things considered, communication in our family is positive and effective.	____	____	____	____

©Copyrighted material. For nonprofit educational purposes only. Not for resale.

American Family Strengths Inventory©

Managing Stress and Crisis Effectively—Composite

After all family members have filled out their individual American Family Strengths Inventories, you then can transfer each person's responses on *Managing Stress and Crisis Effectively* to this Composite form.

After recording your perceptions, spend some enjoyable time talking together about how your views are similar and how they are different. Remember: No one is absolutely right and no one is absolutely wrong on this. Everyone has a valid perception of what is happening and their views need to be considered carefully and respectfully.

Date:_____   **Family Members' Names**

In Our Family ...   ____   ____   ____   ____

A crisis has helped us grow closer together.   ____   ____   ____   ____

It is easy to find solutions to our problems when we talk about them.   ____   ____   ____   ____

It's important to try to change the things that we agree need changing, rather than ignoring the situation.   ____   ____   ____   ____

We can work together to solve very difficult family problems.   ____   ____   ____   ____

A crisis helps make our relationships strong.   ____   ____   ____   ____

We try not to worry too much because things usually work out OK.   ____   ____   ____   ____

We are able to face daily issues confidently.   ____   ____   ____   ____

We like to support each other.   ____   ____   ____   ____

Our friends are there when we need them.   ____   ____   ____   ____

A crisis makes us stick closer together.   ____   ____   ____   ____

We always find something good comes from a crisis.   ____   ____   ____   ____

We find it easy to make changes in our plans to meet changing circumstances.   ____   ____   ____   ____

We have the courage to try to do new things
in life that will improve things for our family.   ____   ____   ____   ____

We can accept things in life that we know
cannot be changed and find peace.   ____   ____   ____   ____

All things considered, we look at challenges
as opportunities for growth.   ____   ____   ____   ____

©Copyrighted material. For non-profit educational purposes only. Not for resale.

American Family Strengths Inventory©

Spiritual Well-being—Composite

After all family members have filled out their individual American Family Strengths Inventories, you then can transfer each person's responses on *Spiritual Well-being* to this Composite form.

After recording your perceptions, spend some enjoyable time talking together about how your views are similar and how they are different. Remember: No one is absolutely right and no one is absolutely wrong on this. Everyone has a valid perception of what is happening and their views need to be considered carefully and respectfully.

Date:_____   **Family Members' Names**

In Our Family ...   ____ ____ ____ ____

We have a hopeful attitude toward life.   ____ ____ ____ ____

Our home feels like a sanctuary to all of us.   ____ ____ ____ ____

We have a strong sense of belonging.   ____ ____ ____ ____

We enjoy learning about our family history.   ____ ____ ____ ____

We feel strong connections with our
ancestors.   ____ ____ ____ ____

There is a feeling of safety and security.   ____ ____ ____ ____

We feel connected with nature and the world
around us.   ____ ____ ____ ____

We feel a strong connection with the land.   ____ ____ ____ ____

There is a sense of peace among us.   ____ ____ ____ ____

We believe that love is a powerful force that   ____ ____ ____ ____
keeps us together.

We benefit in many ways from our belief in a
higher being or power.   ____ ____ ____ ____

It is easy to share our spiritual values and
beliefs with each other.   ____ ____ ____ ____

Our personal religious beliefs are compatible
with each other.   ____   ____   ____   ____

All things considered, we have strong spiri-
tual connections that enhance our well-   ____   ____   ____   ____
being.

©Copyrighted material. For nonprofit educational purposes only. Not for resale.

American Family Strengths Inventory©

Enjoyable Time Together—Composite

After all family members have filled out their individual American Family Strengths Inventories, you then can transfer each person's responses on *Enjoyable Time Together* to this Composite form.

After recording your perceptions, spend some enjoyable time talking together about how your views are similar and how they are different. Remember: No one is absolutely right and no one is absolutely wrong on this. Everyone has a valid perception of what is happening and their views need to be considered carefully and respectfully.

Date:_____

Family Members' Names

In Our Family ...

We have a number of common interests.

We like to have fun together.

We feel comfortable with each other.

We enjoy trying out new activities together.

We enjoy hearing our grandparents' stories about the past.

We enjoy simple, inexpensive family activities.

We like to have a place we call home.

We feel strongly connected to each other.

Hanging out together builds strong relationships.

We have lots of good times together.

We often laugh with each other.

Observing family rituals and customs is important to us.

We enjoy sharing our memories with each other.

We enjoy having unplanned, spontaneous
activities with each other.   ____   ____   ____   ____

All things considered, we have adequate
time for each other, and we enjoy the time we
share together.   ____   ____   ____   ____

©Copyrighted material. For nonprofit educational purposes only. Not for resale.

Global Measures
of the Family's Strengths Composite

After recording your perceptions, spend some enjoyable time talking together about how your views are similar and how they are different. Remember: No one is absolutely right and no one is absolutely wrong on this. Everyone has a valid perception of what is happening and their views need to be considered carefully and respectfully.

Date:_____   **Family Members' Names**

In Our Family ...   _____   _____   _____   _____

    We love one another.   _____   _____   _____   _____

    Life in our family is satisfying to us.   _____   _____   _____   _____

    We are a happy family.   _____   _____   _____   _____

    All things considered, we are a strong family.   _____   _____   _____   _____

©Copyrighted material. For nonprofit educational purposes only. Not for resale.

References

Beavers, W.R., & Hampson, R.B. (1990). *Successful families*. New York: Norton.

Billingsley, A. (1986). *Black families in White America*. Englewood Cliffs, NJ: Prentice Hall. *Building Strong Families: Choices and Challenges*. (1997). Columbia, MO: University of Missouri Outreach and Extension.

Casas, C., Stinnett, N., DeFrain, J., Williams, R., & Lee, P. (1984). Latin American family strengths. *Family Perspective, 18,* 11-17.

Cook, R. (2000). *Discourses inspiring the strengths of a selection of New Zealand families*. Unpublished master's thesis, University of Waikato, Hamilton, New Zealand. Creating a Strong Family. (2005). University of Nebraska–Lincoln UNL for Families Web site: www.UNLforFamilies.unl.edu

Craig, K. (1999). Personal communication.

Curran, D. (1983). *Traits of a healthy family*. Minneapolis: Winston Press.

DeFrain, J., DeFrain, N., & Lepard, J. (1994). Family strengths and challenges in the South Pacific: An exploratory study. *International Journal of the Sociology of the Family, 24* (2), 25-47.

DeFrain, J., Jones, J.E., Skogrand, L., & DeFrain, N. (2003). Surviving and transcending a traumatic childhood: An exploratory study. *Marriage & Family Review, 35* (1/2), 117-146.

DeFrain, J., & Stinnett, N. (2002). Family strengths. In J.J. Ponzetti, et al. (Eds.), *International encyclopedia of marriage and family* (2nd ed.). New York: Macmillan Reference Group, pp. 637-642.

Epstein, N.B., Bishop, D.S., Ryan, C., Miller, L., & Keitner, G. (1993). The McMaster model of family functioning. In F. Walsh (Ed.), *Normal family processes* (pp. 138-160). New York: Guilford Press.

Gabler, J., & Otto, H. (1964). Conceptualization of family strengths in the family life and other professional literature. *Journal of Marriage and the Family, 26*, 221-223.

Geggie, J., DeFrain, J., Hitchcock, S., & Silberberg, S. (2000, June). Family strengths research project. Newcastle, N.S.W., Australia: Family Action Centre, University of Newcastle. Web site: http://www.newcastle.edu.au/centre/fac

Goodman, M. (1986, November). Americans and their money: 1986. *Money*, p. 159.

Kantor, D., & Lehr, W. (1974). *Inside the family*. San Francisco: Jossey-Bass.

Krysan, M., Moore, K.A., & Zill, N. (1990). Identifying successful families: An overview of constructs and selected measures. Washington, DC: Child Trends, Inc. [2100 M St., NW, Suite 610] and the U.S. Department of Health and Human Services, Office of the Assistant Secretary for Planning and Evaluation.

Lingren, H.G., Kimmons, L., Lee, P., Rowe, G., Rottmann, L., Schwab, L., & Williams, R. (1988). *Family strengths 8-9: Pathways to well-being*. Lincoln, NE: Center for Family Strengths, University of Nebraska.

Lykken, D.T. (1999). *Happiness*. New York: Golden Books, p. 17.

Mace, D.R. (2006). In D.H. Olson & J. DeFrain, *Marriages and families: Intimacy, diversity, and strengths* (5th ed.), p. xxi.

Mberengwa, L.R., & Johnson, J.M. (2003). Strengths of Southern African families and their cultural context. *Journal of Family and Consumer Sciences, 95* (1), 20-25.

Moore, K.A., Chalk, R., Scarpa, J., & Vandivere, S. (2002, August). Family strengths: Often overlooked, but real. Child Trends Research Brief [4301 Connecticut Avenue, NW, Suite 100, Washington, DC 20008]. Web site: www.childtrends.org.

National Geographic Society. (1995). *Hong Kong: A family portrait*. Washington, D.C.: National Geographic Video.

Olson, D.H. (1996). Clinical assessment and treatment using the Circumplex Model. In F.W. Kaslow (Ed.), *Handbook in relational diagnosis* (pp. 59-80). New York: Wiley.

Olson, D.H., & DeFrain, J. (2006). *Marriages and families: Intimacy, strengths, and diversity* (5th ed.). Boston: McGraw-Hill.

Olson, D.H., McCubbin, H.I., Barnes, H., Larsen, A., Muxen, M., & Wilson, M. (1989). *Families: What makes them work* (2nd ed.). Los Angeles, CA: Sage.

Otto, H.A. (1962). What is a strong family? *Marriage and Family Living, 24,* 77-81.

Otto, H.A. (1963). Criteria for assessing family strength. *Family Process, 2,* 329-339.

Reiss, D. (1981). *The family's construction of reality.* Cambridge, MA: Harvard University Press.

Rowe, G., DeFrain, J., King, K., Lingren, H., Stinnett, N., Van Zandt, S., & Williams, R. (1984). *Family strengths 5: Continuity and change.* Newton, MA: Education Development Center.

Sani, A., & Buhannad, N. (2003). Family strengths in Islam: Perceptions of women in the United Arab Emirates. National Council on Family Relations *Report, 48* (4), F12-F15.

Stinnett, N., Chesser, B., & DeFrain, J. (eds.). (1979). *Building family strengths: Blueprints for action.* Lincoln, NE: University of Nebraska Press.

Stinnett, N., Chesser, B., DeFrain, J., & Knaub, P. (eds.). (1980). *Family strengths: positive models for family life.* Lincoln, NE: University of Nebraska Press.

Stinnett, N. & Defrain, J. (1985). *Secrets of strong families.* Boston: Little Brown.

Stinnett, N. & O'Donnell, M. (1996). *Good kids.* New York: Doubleday.

Stinnett, N., & Sauer, K. (1977). Relationship characteristics of strong families. *Family Perspective, 11* (3), 3-11.

Whitaker, C. (1975). Personal communication.

Williams, R., Lingren, H., Rowe, G., Van Zandt, S., Lee, P., & Stinnett, N. (1985). *Family strengths 6: Enhancement of interaction.* Lincoln, NE: Department of Human Development and the Family, University of Nebraska.

Woodhouse, C.G. (1930). A study of 250 successful families. *Social Forces, 8,* 511-532.

Xia, Y., Xie, X., & Zhou, Z. (2004). Case study: Resiliency in immigrant families. In V.L. Bengtson, A. Acock, K. Allen, P. Dilworth-Anderson, & D. Klein (Eds.), *Sourcebook of family theory and research* (pp. 108-111). Thousand Oaks, CA: Sage.

Xie, X., DeFrain, J., Meredith, W., & Combs, R. (1996). Family strengths in the People's Republic of China. *International Journal of the Sociology of the Family, 26* (2), 17-27.

Xu, A., & Ye, W. (2002). Quality of marriage: Major predictors of stability. Shanghai *Research Quarterly, 4,* 103-112.

Yoo, Y. J. (2004). A study of the development of the Korean Family Strengths Scale for Strengthening the Family. *Journal of the Korean Association of Family Relations, 9* (2), 119-151.

Yoo, Y. J., DeFrain, J., Lee, I., Kim, S., Hong, S., Choi, H., & Ahn, J. (2004, June). Korean family strengths research project: A national project funded by the Korea Research Foundation. Seoul, Korea: Institute of Korean Family Strengths and Kyunghee University.

Index

978-0-595-45886-8
0-595-45886-6